LANGUAGE AND LITERA...

Dorothy S. Strickland, FOUND...
Celia Genishi and Donna E. Alverma...

(Continued)

---

* Volumes with an asterisk following the title are a part of the NCRLL set: Approaches to Language and Literacy Research, edited by JoBeth Allen and Donna E. Alvermann.

When Commas Meet Kryptonite

Classroom Lessons from the Comic Book Project

MICHAEL BITZ

Forewords by

*Jim Davis and
James Bucky Carter*

Teachers College, Columbia University
New York and London

Published by Teachers College Press, 1234 Amsterdam Avenue, New York, NY 10027

Permissions Acknowledgments:

Selections from *Vampire Loves, Laika, American Born Chinese,* and *Joey Fly Private Eye* are reprinted here (Figures 1.1–1.4) with permission from First Second Books.
Selections from *Wireman* (Figures 2.1–2.2) are reprinted here with permission from the author, Susan Stauffacher.
A selection from *Bleach,* reprinted here (Figure 2.4), is copyrighted by Viz Media.
Selections of student work are reprinted throughout with permission from the respective authors and artists.

Library of Congress Cataloging-in-Publication Data

Bitz, Michael, EdD.
    When commas meet Kryptonite : classroom lessons from the comic book project / Michael Bitz.
        p. cm. — (Language and literacy series)
    Includes bibliographical references and index.
    ISBN 978-0-8077-5065-0 (pbk. : alk. paper)
    ISBN 978-0-8077-5066-7 (hardcover : alk. paper)
    1. Comic books, strips, etc., in education. 2. Language arts. I. Title.
    LB1044.9.C59B58   2010
    372.6′044—dc22   2009046335

ISBN 978-0-8077-5065-0 (paper)
ISBN 978-0-8077-5066-7 (cloth)

Printed on acid-free paper
Manufactured in the United States of America

17 16 15 14 13 12 11 10   8 7 6 5 4 3 2 1

Contents

Foreword:
A Comic Artist on Literacy

I have a favorite picture from my childhood because it more or less foretells my future. I'm 4 years old, sitting on the porch steps at our family farm, and I'm reading a Dick Tracy comic book. "Reading" might be an overstatement—I didn't start reading until first grade—this was, after all, before *Sesame Street*, but it's clear from the grainy

photo that I was actively engaged in the storytelling thanks to the colorful pictures, which, when placed sequentially, were as enlightening as any traditional work of literature.

I grew up loving comics and comic books. I remember impatiently waiting to get my hands on the Sunday funnies so I could read the latest adventures of Steve Canyon, a beautifully crafted strip by Milton Caniff. Through the magic of his pen, I imagined fabulous places far beyond the borders of Fairmount, Indiana.

As a kid, I had asthma, so I had to spend a fair amount of time in bed. My mom would hand me a tablet of paper and a pencil and tell me to entertain myself. And I did. I drew

pictures that were so bad; I had to put labels on them. I'd draw a cow and then label it "cow." I didn't realize it at the time, but I was becoming a cartoonist. Pretty soon, my abilities as an artist improved to the point that I didn't have to label everything, but I found it was easier to make my mom laugh when I combined words and pictures. Sure, she was an easy mark, but her encouragement led me to where I am today—the "owner" of a fat lazy orange cat named Garfield.

Michael Bitz founded the Comic Book Project in 2001 after he heard from numerous parents that comic books helped their child learn to read. I have had a similar experience with Garfield. When you first hear a parent say something like that to you, you're thinking, "I was really just trying to be funny." But, when you hear it a thousand times, you have to start wondering, "What's going on here?" I'm not an educator, but the simple fact is, Garfield gets a child's attention, and that's the first step in the learning process.

I first met Michael Bitz in 2005, and by 2007 we had started a partnership to advance the idea that comics and comic books can help a child learn to read. Michael shared his knowledge and research to help us create the Comics Lab on our Professor Garfield website (www.professorgarfield.org). It's a free website for students with a clear focus on literacy. The Comics Lab invites students to create their own comic strip using characters, backgrounds, speech and thought balloons, props, and more. It requires the student to think in terms of characters, plots, perspective, spelling, grammar, punctuation—in short, many disciplines are employed to complete one task.

Whether you're an educator, writer, illustrator, parent, or a Superman fan who got drawn in by the word "kryptonite" in the title of this book, I know you'll find this work fascinating, relevant, and possibly life changing. Enjoy. I'll see you in the funny pages.

—Jim Davis

Foreword:
A Literacy Educator on Comics

Michael Bitz is a leading scholar among those of us who study the pedagogical potential of comics. Whether this is your first exposure to the amazing work that he has helped young people across the nation create and publish, or if you recognize, as I do, the importance of knowing his entire published milieu, you are in for an exciting, well-informed, and illuminating reading experience packed with examples of authentic learning. I am fond of quoting reading scholar Brian Cambourne's definition of authenticity:

> Authenticity refers to the degree to which learning activities used to promote reading resemble the kinds of reading activities and learning that occur outside the traditional, institutionalized school setting. The more an activity is like an everyday activity, the higher degree of authenticity it possesses. With respect to meaning, writing and other accoutrements of literacy, the more that an activity requires students to engage in the kind of reading-writing-literacy behaviors that highly literate, proficient adults use to address their needs, the more authentic the activity is judged to be. (2002, p. 38)

As you read this book, you will note how students engage in every aspect of the writing process. You will see them develop critical thinking skills, increase their cultural and self-knowledge, and advance multiple literacy skills as they metacognitively focus on every aspect of composing excellent stories via comics art. You will notice them deciding how to illustrate tone via linguistic or visual markers and how to best punctuate a sentence for maximum dramatic affect and reader comprehension. You will see them consider how color and framing speak to a reader without saying a word. They will share their thoughts on how best to make a work public once it is complete. All the while, the students in the Comic Book Project (CBP) bridge the divide between school-based concepts of excellence, composition, and publication and notions rooted *in their own* senses of purpose and desires to communicate. The results are exemplary blends of learning the *complete* English language arts, which NCTE and IRA (1996) jointly define as reading, writing, listening, speaking, visualizing, and visually representing. The best part? Their work is largely self-directed and stems from their own motivations to do well.

Of course, in many schools across the nation, finding such authentic learning experiences during school can be difficult. Stringent curricula and conservative notions of knowledge and how to measure it often strangle creativity and crumble the bridge between school and real life before it can be built. Dr. Bitz, aware of this frustrating reality, has crafted this text with suggestions on how practicing teachers can most successfully integrate CBP strategies into their classes. Those not familiar with comics will immediately have access to an easy-to-understand primer on their elements and their history regarding education. Every chapter includes activities for application grounded in the best of currently researched and well-regarded classroom practices, such as scaffolding, group work, assessment, community building, linguistic exploration, reading development, and process-based composition. A fluid writing style matches the well-informed chapters. While few books in education qualify as page turners, teachers eager to integrate authentic instruction and student-centered activities in their classes will find the book hard to put down.

I wrote of Dr. Bitz's recent book, *Manga High* (2009a), which offered the most compelling evidence to date for teachers to consider comics in their classrooms (Carter, 2009). *When Commas Meet Kryptonite* expands that evidence and situates CBP learning within the framework of the English language arts and multiple literacies. It offers teachers clearly articulated and well-crafted activities for building bridges of authenticity that are built on the foundations of evidence and stirring, self-directed student results.

—James Bucky Carter

Acknowledgments

There are far too many people and organizations to acknowledge for their support of the Comic Book Project, so thank you to all of the educators and students who have helped to transform the project from an idea to a reality to a creative movement. The Center for Arts Education Research at Teachers College, Columbia University—led by Professors Judy Burton and Harold Abeles—graciously hosted the Comic Book Project from 2004 to 2008. Dark Horse Comics shared a vision for the project from the very beginning. Many thanks to the staff, board, and friends of the Mind Trust for the fellowship in educational entrepreneurship. Thank you to the faculty, administration, and students at Ramapo College of New Jersey. The After-School Corporation (TASC) in New York City was the first to pilot the Comic Book Project and has remained a dedicated supporter.

Thank you to the following people who have supported me: Bill McKinney, Andre Worrell, Susan Robeson, Barbara Salander, Carmen Colon, Doug Tarnopol, Masami Toku, Lori Campos, Carol Kerney, Margaret Akin, Marge Pellegrino, Patrick McLaughlin, Brent Wilson, Shaila Mulholland, Tom Kurzanski, Dan Jeselsohn, Phil DeJean, Rebecca Fabiano, Patricia Ayala, Jim Davis, Bob Levy, Larry Smith, James Bucky Carter, Jennifer Stark, Adam Rabiner, Mike Dogan, Margaret Hagood, Karen Clark-Keys, Sandra Noble, Sherri Pittard, Peter Guttmacher, Randall Glenn, Aaron Dworkin, Barbara Ferman, Catie Cavanaugh, Meg Lemke, Pat Donohue, Kevin McGowan, Brenda Manuelito, Alissa Torres, Danny Anker, Fern Eisgrub, Fabian Leo, Francoise Mouly, Gina Gagliano, Sara Hill, John Merrow, James Sturm, Michelle Ollie, Pernell Brice, Lena Townsend, and Scott Cabot.

A special thank you to my family, especially my wife, Allison, for all their support.

Comic Books in Education

I estimate 500—the number of adults who have approached me and gushed, "Comic books taught me how to read!" For most of these people and many others, difficulty with literacy acquisition made reading more than a chore. This put up a serious barrier to learning and success in school. Then these struggling readers discovered comic books, the "ninth art."* The superheroes leapt into their imaginations, the stories engrossed them, and the students were hooked. And they were *reading*. With each ensuing issue of *Spider-Man* or *Batman*, they began to connect how words and language supported and completed the drawn narratives—and vice versa. Their favorite characters were speaking in those familiar cartoon bubbles, and the young comic book enthusiasts wanted to know what the valiant superheroes and reviled villains were saying. The children dusted off their dictionaries when a caption in *The Mighty Avengers*, for example, referred to a planet as a "barren orb" (Stern, 1984, p. 10). These students were absorbing extremely advanced vocabulary—more than if they had been watching television, reading a children's book, or conversing with an adult (Hayes & Ahrens, 1988).

Amazingly, most of the people who tell me they learned to read from comic books had to do so in secret. Their parents and teachers wanted them to read "real" books. Comic books were a diversion at best; at worst they denigrated not only language and literature but also children's moral fiber. In the 1950s, this was serious business. The psychologist Fredric Wertham wrote *Seduction of the Innocent* (1954), which blamed comic books for the ruin of American youth. Congress even held hearings into the relationship between comic books and juvenile delinquency (see U.S. Congress, 1955). Many readers have described to me how they concealed their comic books

---

* The term *ninth art* originates from French author Claude Beylie's extension of *Manifesto of the Seven Arts* by Italian film theoretician Ricciotto Canudo. Canudo (1923) developed a list of the seven most important arts; architecture was first and cinema seventh. Beylie (1964) added the eighth and ninth, television and comics.

from adults. Some hid comics under their pillows or in empty suitcases. In school the comics were slipped between the pages of textbooks or poetry readers. When the teacher turned her back to write on the board, the students flipped past Robert Frost and Emily Dickinson to John Broome and Gil Kane (1959):

> In brightest day, in blackest night,
> No evil shall escape my sight!
> Let those who worship evil's might,
> Beware my power . . . Green Lantern's light!

WHY COMIC BOOKS AND WHY NOW?

Through the 20th century, comic books remained disparaged in and out of the classroom, even though the comics publishing industry attempted to change its image through the "Comics Code," a series of self-imposed regulations regarding violent and sexual content (Nyberg, 1998). The policies did little to change public perception. Comics publisher Françoise Mouly (2009) recounted her first attempts to publish Art Spiegelman's *Maus* in the 1980s: "The idea of a comic book about the Holocaust was outrageous; to most people it was sacrilegious" (p. ix). The scorn of comics as a form and the surreptitious nature of comic book reading, spanning decades of young enthusiasts, highlight the dichotomy between the books that teachers assign and those that children choose to read. Sitting in a dark closet, the child with a flashlight shining on Captain America is a prime example of recreational reading, or what the literacy researcher Stephen Krashen (2004) has dubbed Free Voluntary Reading (FRV). Not surprisingly, the amount of time that children spend reading for pleasure is the primary indicator of their reading competence, vocabulary level, and ability to understand complex grammatical constructions. Hence, what excuse is there for a teacher, and schooling as a whole, to ignore the books chosen by children? Comics offer an opportunity for literacy building and a bridge to more conventional literature.

The call by educational researchers, theorists, and writers to make schooling more personally and socially relevant is nothing new. Throughout the 20th century, John Dewey advocated for meaningful education centered on children and their personal experiences. His arguments for progressive education continue to reverberate in today's debate on the nature and purpose of education. He wrote in *Experience and Education* (1998):

> There is, I think, no point in the philosophy of progressive education which is sounder than its emphasis upon the importance of the participation of the learner in the formation of the purposes which direct his activities in the learning process, just as there is no defect in traditional education greater than its failure to secure the active co-operation of the pupil in construction of the purposes involved in his studying. (p. 77)

Academics through the years have piggybacked on Dewey's call for relevant education, oftentimes through the exploration of popular and youth culture as fodder for learning activities. Flood, Heath, and Lapp (1997, 2008) collected voluminous amounts of research and writing that explored the literacy implications of everything from anime fanfiction to punk rock zines. Anne Haas Dyson (1993, 1997, 2003) has explored young children's literacy use in the context of their participation in popular culture (including comic books). Yet even a person with no classroom experience can imagine the slippery pedagogical slope of teaching through popular texts or youth media. Donna Alvermann, Jennifer Moon, and Margaret Hagood (1999) and David Buckingham (1998)—some of the most avid proponents of media literacy and education in traditional classrooms—all concede the challenges that popular culture introduces into an educational setting. Buckingham, for example, cites a study by Grace and Tobin (1998), which examined a media project at an elementary school in Hawaii; the students' self-produced videos emulated the raunchy cartoon *Beavis and Butthead*, much to consternation of teachers, parents, and administrators. But Buckingham (along with many others) also recognizes some extraordinary possibilities for popular culture in the classroom, predicated on the teacher's and students' development of a popular media *metalanguage*: "a form of critical discourse in which to describe and analyze what is taking place" (Buckingham, 2003, p. 325).

Specific to comics, many have championed the use of comics as motivational pathways to reading (Anderson & Styles, 1999; Dorrell, 1987; Dorrell & Carroll, 1981; Goldstein, 1986; Thomas, 1983; Wright, 1979). More recently advocates have highlighted *manga* (Japanese comic books) as a reading tool (Allen & Ingulsrud, 2005; Schwartz & Rubinstein-Avila, 2006). Others promote graphic novels, which are longer comic books published in a single perfect-bound volume (like a novel) rather than serialized, magazine-style issues (Bucher & Manning, 2004; Crawford, 2004; Mac-Donald, 2004; O'English, Matthews, & Lindsay, 2006). Some proponents also define graphic novels as more "literary" in value than comic books. The term is used to market them as such by mainstream publishers, and graphic novels are sold in bookstores as often as in specialized comic book shops. However, many critically acclaimed graphic novels were first serialized as comic books.

Of course, appeals from the ivory tower do not always influence classroom practice, and comic books have been mostly shunned by the educational establishment . . . until recently. A rapidly growing movement of K–12 educators is embracing comics as a form of literature and a pathway to reading and writing. Interestingly, the comics-in-education movement is led by neither English language arts teachers nor visual arts teachers; rather, it is spearheaded by librarians. Librarians have consistently sought new ways to engage children in reading, so it is no surprise that comics first made their way into schools via the library. Graphic novels in particular lined both school and public library shelves when the Pulitzer Prize was awarded to Art Spiegelman (2003) for the second volume of his graphic novel *Maus*, which recounts his father's experiences during the Holocaust. The trend has continued with numerous graphic novels based on historical and cultural events, including Marjane Satrapi's *Persepolis* (2003), a memoir of growing up in Iran during the Islamic Revolution. The Young Adult Library Services Association produces an annual list, "Great Graphic Novels for Teens," ranging from such nonfiction as *The United States Constitution: A Graphic Adaptation* (Hennessey & McConnell, 2008) to humorous fiction such as *The Plain Janes* (Castellucci & Rugg, 2007). As a testament to librarians' acceptance of the medium, the American Library Association (2008) has added to its intellectual freedom policies a section titled "Dealing with Challenges to Graphic Novels."

Beyond the library, teachers across the United States and around the world are examining the comic book medium as a viable educational tool. Many of these teachers are themselves avid comics readers. A prime example is Scott Cabot, a high school social studies teacher in New York City. As a child Cabot cherished the canon of classic comic books, beginning with DC Comics and then Marvel. As an educator he has used comics and graphic novels to teach historical themes. Cabot is so passionate about the value of comics as a teaching tool that he undertook the daunting mound of paperwork necessary to establish Siegel and Schuster High School, named after the creators of Superman. This school would use comics as a basis for learning in every subject area in every period of the school day. The New York City Department of Education rejected his proposal in 2007, but Cabot plans to reapply.

Yet for many educators—particularly English language arts teachers who grew up reading conventional books as opposed to comic books—

the world of comic books and graphic novels is still very much a mystery. How do those rectangular boxes on the page represent a logical sequence? What connections can be made to sentence structure and writing mechanics? Why are children—boys and girls alike—so engaged in these texts? What is it about the characters, stories, and very essence of a comic book that draws in readers who may be loath to read or write a paragraph?

This book aims to answer these questions. My goal is to provide educators with a broad base of knowledge and understanding of comics in the classroom so that they will be able to embrace this medium as a form of literature and, in doing so, connect with students in unique and socially relevant ways. Readers should know that I—perhaps like many of them—did *not* grow up reading comics. I came to understand and appreciate the form by observing positive literacy experiences that elementary and secondary students were having with comic books, as well as by exploring the pathways to creativity via the process of children designing original comic books. As an educator I aim to find any and every way to engage children not just in words and language but in learning as a life pursuit. While certainly not the only opportunity for student engagement in the curricular spectrum, comics are a unique tool for developing essential literacy skills and can provide an inspiration for further learning.

INTRODUCING THE COMIC BOOK PROJECT

This book is largely drawn upon the experiences of students and teachers who have participated in the Comic Book Project (CBP), a national literacy initiative that I founded in 2001. I write about CBP throughout this book, and the student-generated comic books that conclude each chapter resulted from many months of effort on the part of some extremely dedicated educators and learners. The mission of CBP is to engage young people in the process of drafting, writing, and designing original comic books, which we then publish and present to other youths as learning and motivational tools. It is important to note that CBP has never focused on creating comics the "right" way, Marvel way, manga way, or any other predetermined way. Rather, the comic books that children create are a conduit for creativity, critical thinking, identity exploration, and community engagement. CBP encompasses children of all abilities, backgrounds, and interests, not just those who consider themselves artists or comics readers. The program began with a single middle school in New York City and has since reached over 50,000 children across the United States and internationally.

The experiences of resilient educators and determined students highlight the educational vigor of comic books beyond colorful pages and action-based stories. The process of creating a comic book requires children to reflect upon personal experiences and identities within the context of an original sequential narrative. In doing so, children need to contemplate elements of character trait; plot line; tone and atmosphere; foreshadowing and inference; and, of course, spelling, grammar, and punctuation. They also need to consider artistic elements of character design; foreground and background; color; perspective; and the font of written texts. However, most of the educators involved with CBP never considered themselves artists and have little personal connection to comics as literature. Their success is a true testament to the power of creativity in learning and the importance of engaging children in authentic, meaningful learning experiences.

ABOUT THIS BOOK

This book is divided into chapters representing core literacy skills and practices reinforced by comics. But more specifically, the volume is focused on the learning opportunities presented by writing, creating, and sharing original comics in an educational setting. There are a number of quality resources related to professionally published comics as a pathway to reading, including Booth and Lundy (2007), Carter (2007), Cary (2004), Frey and Fisher (2008), and Gorman (2003). But why stop with stocking your library? Why not employ comic books (and other forms of youth media and culture) in the context of a comprehensive and authentic literacy approach that includes writing, listening, speaking, editing, revising, sharing, and publishing? Why not give children a voice in the learning process by helping them to develop their own characters, storylines, conflicts, and resolutions? Why not help teachers become instructional designers, parents become mentors, and community members become support systems for students who rarely picture themselves as accomplished authors and artists?

The chapters of this book focus on elements of process and product—how students go from blank paper to written manuscripts to artfully developed comic books to published compilations of student work. Each chapter concludes with a relevant classroom activity that teachers can modify for the needs of their students and learning goals. I also offer suggestions for classroom resources, including comic books, graphic novels, websites, and other media. Also, chapters contain many examples from student work, among them eight annotated student-created comic books by youths across the United States, from New York to Hawaii. These examples can be used to inspire your students, as you develop your own portfolio of exemplary student work. As you read these student examples, think about the process that resulted in these products, and then imagine how that process would play out in your classroom. Full-color versions of the student publications cited in this book, and many more, are available as free downloads at www. ComicBookProject.org. Every one of these comic book stories is enveloped by another, more important, story: that of the children and teachers who created these exemplary works of literature. Hence, embedded into the discussion of literacy skills, classroom organization, and lesson plan development is a narrative about CBP. A large part of this story relates to teachers, students, and communities—all in underserved areas—who adapted a simple curricular model to accomplish unique and extraordinary things with some paper, pencils, and ideas. These stories remind us that superheroes may not come to the aid of struggling readers and writers, but children themselves become heroic when they harness the power of creativity and use that power to teach the rest of us important lessons about literacy and life.

CHAPTER 1

What *Are* Comics?

"When I was a little kid I knew *exactly* what comics were," writes Scott McCloud in the opening of his seminal *Understanding Comics: The Invisible Art* (1993, p. 2). He proceeds to dissect the comics medium from the perspective of a professional artist and comics enthusiast. This thorough analysis of the composition of comics, alongside McCloud's personal experiences as an avid comics fan and artist, is a rich resource for answering the question, What *are* comics? Another resource for deconstructing the medium is comics legend Will Eisner's *Comics and Sequential Art* (1985). As Eisner writes, "In its most economical state, comics employ a series of repetitive images and recognizable symbols. When these are used again and again to convey similar ideas, they become a language—a literary form, if you will" (p. 8). Eisner's analytical work considers comics within the contexts of literacy, psychology, and anthropology. He even peered ahead decades into the future to accurately predict how technology and computers would affect comics as an art form and a business. In fact, whereas comics scholarship was once a limited field at best, there are now numerous valuable resources available for "understanding comics," including books (Heer & Worcester, 2009; Versaci, 2007; Wolk, 2008), websites, journals, conferences, and dissertations.

But, these works of "comics literary theory" may leave many educators scratching their heads and searching for practical applications in their own classrooms. Most educators are neither professional artists nor comic book enthusiasts.

This book is designed to answer the needs of those readers. This chapter provides a simple deconstruction of comics from an educator's perspective, to enable teachers to quickly understand how comics are viable in their classrooms.

A NOTE ABOUT TERMS

A most mystifying issue for many educators is the variety of terms used to describe the subject of this book: *comics, comic books, comic strips, cartoons, graphic novels, manga.* The different terms originated with new forms that have arisen over the years. *Cartoons* originally appeared in newspapers at the end of the 19th century as a way to build readership and comment on news of the day. Cartoons usually featured text woven into the illustration. It was Rudolph Dirk's cartoon *Katzenjammer Kids* in the *Journal American* that first placed speech in the now familiar word balloons. Once those characters began to speak, they had more to say—leading to the *comic strip* (*comic* because they were meant to be funny). Comic strips featured a few pictures in a row in order to tell a mini-story. Unlike most of today's comic strips, the early strips were "serialized," meaning that the story would continue in the next issue of the newspaper.

The ongoing stories put forth by comic strips naturally transformed into *comic books*, which appeared en masse with the development of new printing processes shortly after the Great Depression. Like the early comic strips, comic books were serialized. Readers would anxiously wait for the next issue in order to know what happened to their favorite characters like Superman and Spider-Man. Most of these stories were no longer humorous, but the *comics* moniker remained. *Graphic novels*, a more recent invention, are essentially comic books in novel-length form. Just as the first comic books began as collections of comic strips, the earliest graphic novels began as collections of comic books. Most graphic novels are not serialized, but some are, among them Jeff Smith's *Bone* (2005), which began as a comic book series. Finally, *manga* are Japanese-style comic books. Manga has as rich a history as American comic books, and manga has become a worldwide phenomenon in recent years.

With all that said, everything described above (with the exception of cartoons) falls under the umbrella of *comics.* The term *comics* refers to the medium, and all else—comic books, graphic novels, manga, and so on—are forms of the medium. In this book, when I refer to *comics,* I include everything within the medium; otherwise, I distinguish between the forms by referring specifically to a *comic book* or *graphic novel.*

So just what *are* comics?

INTRODUCING SEQUENTIAL ARTISTIC-WRITTEN NARRATIVES (AKA COMICS)

Comics are a vehicle for narrative. Quite obviously a comic book is a *book.* It has a front cover, back cover, and numerous printed pages in between. We "read," rather than view, watch, or play, comics. In this regard comics are more closely aligned with traditional educational materials than most other popular media—much more so than videogames, trading cards, or popular music. In the context of new media and literacies, comics are a rare bridge between the canon of reading skills that children are expected to master in school and the literacies that they embrace on their own and out of school. I was reminded of this the last time I visited a large bookstore in New York City around 4:00 p.m. The store was filled with youths, many causing havoc in the philosophy and cookbook aisles. But the section of comic books, manga, and graphic novels was lined with children—boys and girls—silently and voraciously reading book after book after book.

Structurally, most comic books and graphic novels are much like conventional books, at least in the genre of fiction. They are typically sequential narratives. Both engage the reader with an opening, which sets the stage for the story. We get a sense of the tone and atmosphere from this opening, and we are usually introduced to the main characters. In Figure 1.1, from *Vampire Loves* (Sfar, 2006), for example, we see an eerie castle backed by spindly trees and a half moon, a perfect setting for the main character, Ferdinand the Vampire. Then we are led through a series of events, circumstances, and conflicts, which follow a logical order. Ferdinand hears a mysterious knock on the door—it is his ex-girlfriend Lani (a girl/plant), who wants to rekindle their relationship. As the narrative continues, we naturally attempt to predict what will happen next in the sequence. Will Ferdinand take Lani back? In the best books of any genre, we are delightfully surprised when our predictions are erroneous and the story sets our imaginations in many directions. The pages go by, and the story comes to a close with a conclusion. Of course, serialized comic books do not end conclusively, as another addition to the series will appear next month. The student-generated comic book featured in this chapter concludes with foreboding words: "And the earth was once again at peace . . . but for how long??"

The main difference between comics and traditional books is that comics are not only written narratives—they are also visually artistic narratives. One might wonder why creators of comics do not simply forego the written text and follow the adage "A picture is worth a thousand words." Why not convey their narratives exclusively through interesting and exciting visual art? The Flemish wood engraver Frans Masereel, for example, created narratives through series of woodcuts, including the 1926 work titled *Passionate Journey: A Novel in 165 Woodcuts*. A more recent example is the work of Eric Drooker, creator of *Blood Song* (2002a) and *Flood!* (2002b). These "novels in pictures," as Drooker describes them, begin with an introduction of setting, characters, and conflicts; they follow a logical

Figure 1.1. Excerpted with permission from *Vampire Loves* (2006), by Joann Sfar, First Second Books

sequence; and they conclude with a resolution of themes and ideas. Drooker accomplishes all this through dramatic and breathtaking etchings in black scratchboard, without a single written word.

Yet these examples and other wordless books fall outside the norm of the comics tradition. In general, comics are sequential artistic-written narratives; written words are integral to the comics medium. Comics are a marriage between words and pictures, and the reader must take both into account to fully understand and appreciate the narrative. How readers negotiate the relationship between words and pictures likely depends on the readers themselves. Personally, when I read a comic, I usually take in the written caption or dialogue before I study the picture. Others absorb the picture first, then read the words. Most of us will go back and forth between the words and the pictures—what theorists call "transmediation," or the translation of content and ideas from one form to another (Siegel, 1995; Suhor, 1984).

Although there is little prior research or theory on how children read comics, there is extensive scholarship on a comparable genre with which most literacy educators are very familiar: children's picture books. Like comics, picture books wed written text and visual imagery in a natural and cohesive manner. Lawrence Sipe (2008), a researcher of children's literature, thoroughly examined the interplay between words and pictures in a picture book, and his ideas can be readily applied to comics. Sipe described a text-picture synergy that produces an effect greater than that which text or pictures would create on their own. He cited the work of numerous scholars who attempted to depict the relationships between text and imagery in a picture book, ranging from the idea that pictures extend the text (Schwarcz, 1982) to the concept that pictures and text limit each other (Nodelman, 1988). Sipe concluded, "As readers/viewers, we are always interpreting the words in terms of the pictures and the pictures in terms of the words. . . . The best and most fruitful readings of picturebooks are never straightforwardly linear, but rather involve a lot of reading, turning to previous pages, reviewing, slowing down, and reinterpreting" (p. 27). The same can be safely said for comics.

While, as noted, comics are defined in *this* book as "bound pages," teachers who elect to use technology as the core of their comics initiative might want to investigate the world of web comics, discussed in depth in Chapter 6. Web comics are sequential artistic-written narratives that use the nonlinear aspect of web media to create a new breed in the medium (see http://e-merl.com/pocom.htm as one excellent example). McCloud (2009) explored the concept of the "infinite canvas" in relation to web comics, breaking free from the structured confines of a printed book. An infinite canvas means that the story could continue for as long as the creator desires, unencumbered by page counts or other limitations of printed books. Furthermore, readers do not necessarily have to follow a determined sequence of pages or panels—they can move forward, backward, up, down, or even diagonally within the canvas. Obviously, this type of comic is very different from conventional comics, but web comics are likely the wave of the future, since they allow for a broader creative palette and do not entail expensive printing costs.

CONNECTIONS TO CLASSROOM LITERACY

Making Meaning

Part of the reason why comics involve so much reading, reviewing, and reinterpreting—arguably much more so than a child's picture book—is that the sequential artistic-written narrative of a comic is so varied, albeit through a simple concept of frames, or panels. Figure 1.2 shows a page from a comic book. How do we construct meaning from this form? And more important for improving literacy learning, how do young readers make meaning from it? Fortunately, the panels are outlined; they become windows into the overall narrative. As we are accustomed to reading from top to bottom and left to right, we begin with the panel on the top-left of the page.* Then a decision has to be made about which panel comes next—the panel to the right or the one below? The logical sequence of the story dictates that the panel to the right comes first: the detective interviews the prospective crime fighter before deciding to give him a chance. Between the panels the reader makes an inference that the detective Joey Fly is more than a little proud of himself and that the new young detective is energetic but naive.

This nonlinear decoding process in combination with the text-art synergy makes reading comics intriguing and (gasp!) fun. But there is one aspect of the sequential artistic-written narrative that is more important than the sequence, visual art, or written words: the *narrative*. Comics are built on great stories, timeless characters, and gripping plots. It is the narratives themselves that are the substance of comics. Just like the words in a conventional book, the words and art in a comic are semiotics (signs and symbols) that convey a narrative. Of course, we want children to be able to understand sentence structure and differentiate between an adjective and

---

* Manga translated from its original Japanese reads right to left. See Chapter 2 for more on manga.

Figure 1.2. Excerpted with permission from *Joey Fly Private Eye in Creepy Crawly Time* (2009), by Aaron Reynolds and Neil Numberman, First Second Books

adverb, but we do so for the eventual purpose of communicating ideas and expressing feelings. Will Eisner (1996) dedicated an entire book to the importance of narrative in comics. Similarly, Jim Davis, creator of *Garfield*, once said to me that every day he sits at his drafting table not to write a comic strip but to write a story. This dedicated emphasis on narrative is perhaps the most convincing reason why comics have a purpose and place in literacy building.

Words and Word Art

Words in comics usually appear in either a caption or a word balloon. Captions describe a scene or provide a context for the visual image. Word balloons, on the other hand, put forth dialogue directly from a character's mouth. Sometimes a panel will include both a caption and a word balloon. Caption boxes and word balloons frame the words, but these delineations do more than provide an outline. They reduce verbiage. One would never see in a comic book, "Superman said in an angry tone . . ." Through a word balloon, the reader digests the character's dialogue directly. The anger is expressed in Superman's expression (possibly emotive lines emanating from his head). Captions serve a similar goal of immediately describing the scene without superfluous phrases or literacy devices. Furthermore, the artistic design of a word balloon can aid in conveying meaning of the words. Figure 1.3 highlights this nicely. Even if the reader were unsure of the exact meanings of the words, the jagged edges of the word balloon establish anger in the character's voice.

Figure 1.3.
Excerpted with permission from
Laika **(2007), by Nick Abadzis,**
First Second Books

The writing in comics is almost always concise and simple. More than a few brief sentences would overpower the artwork and disrupt the overall narrative. Therefore, the medium affords support to readers who struggle with the sea of words typical of a conventional paragraph-based book, or those who may be new to English. For educators who are tied to readability ratings such as the Fry Readability Formula (Fry, 1968) or the Flesch-Kincaid Readability Formula (Kincaid, Fishburne, Rogers, & Chissom, 1975), most comics (e.g., *Archie*) are not going to rate very highly, although select ones (e.g., *Ghost in the Shell*) will top the charts (Krashen, 2004; Wright, 1979). Regardless, Szymusiak and Sibberson (2001) reinforce the importance of educators to think beyond "leveled books" based on readability alone; we must acknowledge that students' interests and motivations also play a role in their willingness to eventually read books that are more difficult than current levels of performance. This is particularly true for middle and high school students (Allington, 2002).

The motivational aspect of comics has much to do with "text-picture synergy" (Sipe, 2008). But the synergy goes beyond the distinct semiotics of texts and pictures. Oftentimes, the words themselves are illustrated in a comic book. Figure 1.4 is an example. The word "flash" in the second panel represents the transformation of the characters in the first panel to those in the third. The big block letters, exaggerated font, and increasing size of the letters all reinforce the magnitude of the event. We might call this "word art"—a concept that extends to the illuminated manuscripts of the Middle Ages. The illustration of the word helps to convey the word's meaning in a specific context. Not every word in a comic book is illustrated in this way, but creators do make frequent use of boldface and italics to convey meaning beyond the words themselves.

Through word art and varied typefaces, readers get additional visual clues to the meaning of the text. Beyond reading "road signs," however, there is a psychological basis for the visualization of words as an integral part of the reading process. Howard Gardner argued in *Frames of Mind: The Theory of Multiple Intelligences* (1983) that humans boast several intelligences (e.g., musical and spatial) rather than a single intelligence indicated by a person's IQ. As Gardner noted in his introduction to the 1993 edition of the book, intelligences "are always expressed in the context of specific tasks, domains, and disciplines" (p. xvi), which almost always entail more than one of the intelligences. For example, the task of playing tennis comprises bodily kinesthetic intelligence (to run and then hit the ball) and visual-spatial intelligence (to visualize the court and aim the ball). A tennis game

**Figure 1.4. Excerpted with permission from *American Born Chinese*
(2006), by Gene Luen Yang, First Second Books**

also requires interpersonal intelligence for playing the game fairly and not
being a sore loser. Similarly, the task, domain, and discipline of reading
entail not only verbal-linguistic intelligence (to understand the text), but
also visual-spatial intelligence (to see the words and mentally manipulate
them). The enhanced visual aspect of words in comics helps balance the
linguistic and visual intelligences required for reading, particularly for visual learners and thinkers.

Life of a Comic Book Panel

In deconstructing comics, it is important to take a close examination of the primary structure of the medium—the rectangular boxes, or panels, that fill the pages. From a visual perspective, a single panel in a comic is much like a camera shot in a movie, defined as "a single piece of film imagery without interruptions or editing" (Manchel, 1990, p. 2235). When peering into a movie camera, the cameraperson captures images within a rectangular frame; the eventual moviegoer sees those captured images on another rectangular frame in the form of a movie screen. These frames, parallel in comics and movies, are essential in establishing the "cinematic space" in which a viewer is drawn into the story and then released once the story ends.

For most movie directors, camera shots are well planned long before a camera enters the set, or before the set is even built. The director has many elements to consider in any given camera shot: movement, lighting, color, weight, balance, perspective, range, angle, line of action, and likely many more. The creator of comics must consider these same elements in the design of a panel. Just as the various cinematic camera shots compose a scene that combines with other scenes to form a movie, the various panels compose a page (or folio) that combines with other pages to form a comic. It is no surprise that many directors "storyboard" their movies to plan the camera shots in every scene. These storyboards look very much like panels in comics, in fact.

Using the first three panels of Figure 1.1 as an example, one can imagine how the opening of this comic might play out in the camera shots of a movie scene.

FADE IN:

[Camera Shot # 1]

EXT. SCARY NIGHT SETTING—
LOTS OF BATS AND STRANGE SOUNDS.

Focus on a distant castle in the fog.

EXTERNAL SOUND

Knock! Knock!

[Camera Shot #2]

FERDINAND THE VAMPIRE, a diminutive, nervous vampire—
immediately likeable—dressed in formal tails. Ferdinand looks
out the window with apprehension.

[Camera Shot #3]

PULL BACK ON INSIDE OF CASTLE

Candlelight illuminates a complex spiral staircase and gothic architecture. Ferdinand floats toward the large wooden front door.

FERDINAND

Who could it be?

From a literacy perspective, a comics panel is akin to a paragraph. Both are formations within a contained space but on their own do not convey an entire narrative. A paragraph uses syntax, or sentences, to intertwine setting, character description, dialogue, and other narrative elements. After the final sentence of a paragraph, the reader takes a proverbial or physical breath before continuing on to the next paragraph in the story. There is a moment of reflection during which the reader examines the cues provided by the text about the direction of the overall narrative (Bond & Hayes, 1984; Goldman, Saul, & Coté, 1995). A comics panel is similar, except that information is communicated via visual art in coordination with written text. Then after taking in a comic book panel and everything it entails (tone, atmosphere, imagery, text), readers take a breath. They consider how that panel affects the overall narrative before moving to the next. As discussed earlier in relation to research on picture books, this process involves extensive previewing, scanning, and reviewing.

Again using Figure 1.1 as the example, we can imagine how these three panels could transpire in the paragraphs of a novel.

It was a dark and dreary night outside the castle. The tall, spindly trees stood in the shadows of a thin moon. Even the bats seemed reluctant to be out on such a night, as they scurried about the deep crevices of the castle. Suddenly, a loud sound echoed through the hills: KNOCK! KNOCK!

Ferdinand the Vampire was afraid. His thin frame, dressed in a long tuxedo and knotted tie, moved toward the window of his bedroom. His small ears twitched; his large eyes peered into the night. He stood in silence.

Floating through the air, Ferdinand finally worked up the courage to answer the knock at the door. He floated down the long spiral staircase and under the cobwebbed arches of the castle until he reached the large wooden door set into massive stones. "Who could it be?" he asked aloud.

Details, Details, Details

While we often focus children on reading for the main idea and basic comprehension of a text, the most intriguing aspect of literature of any type is often in the details. For example, in Figure 1.1, there are a number of details that help us understand the nature of Ferdinand the Vampire. The artist puts a nervous expression on the first appearance of Ferdinand's face. His facial expression turns to shock when his ex-girlfriend appears at the door. These visual details are accompanied by clues in the written text. The first adjective used to describe Ferdinand is "afraid." Rather than approaching the door in anger at the disturbance late at night, he is full of apprehension. The culmination of all these details encourages the reader to sympathize with Ferdinand, who is a stark contrast to the typical persona of a vampire.

Not surprisingly, high-quality student-generated comics also take full advantage of the power of details. Take Figure 1.5 as an example. In this comic book Roy's experiment goes awry, and the studious scientist becomes a masked superhero. Can you find the detail in the picture that foreshadows the experiment's malfunction? Just beneath Roy's outstretched right hand are two disconnected plugs—a small, seemingly innocuous mistake that alters the universe forever. Had the reader not noticed this detail, the story would still make sense. But readers who do take in this detail want to warn Roy about the error. They might clench their fists in expectation or

Figure 1.5. Fernando Acevado (fifth grade), PS 89Q, New York City

hold their breaths. They may even call out to Roy, knowing well that the character in the comic book cannot hear them. There is only one reason why the reader would have these reactions: deep engagement in literature. The details facilitate this engagement by helping the reader connect with the author's intentions.

LESSONS FROM THE COMIC BOOK PROJECT

As I learned from experience, it is much easier to deconstruct comics in theory than it is to help children create them from scratch in a classroom setting. As I wrote in *Teachers & Writers* (Bitz, 2008b), the first CBP group of fifth and sixth graders in New York City struggled with how to just start thinking about writing and designing comic books. Fortunately, the children were creative problem solvers, and they came up with some ideas.

One said, "We need characters, like a good guy and a bad guy."

Another said, "It needs a cool story. Let's make it scary!"

A girl in the back said shyly, "But there has to be a lot of good art, and I can't draw."

A boy's eyes lit up as he shouted, "Hey, let's print our comic books and make a million dollars!"

Those four elements—character design, plot development, creative art and layout, and publishing for an audience—provide a strong backbone for any classroom comics initiative. Of course, teachers can adapt instruction in these elements to the needs of their student populations so that these four "quadrants" evolve in different ways. Some teachers elect to have their students work as a large group to collectively develop the characters and storyline before each of the students develops his or her own comic book based on what the entire class had planned. In contrast, other teachers divide students into teams of three or four, each with a writer, artist, and editor. Occasionally the youths switch roles during the process, and sometimes a particular writer or artist fills in with another group that finds itself stalled or in need of additional support. Demonstrating yet another model, some teachers have each student be responsible for a single panel of the school's comic book; as a group they weave together the panels of their sequential artistic-written narrative like a literary quilt.

Regardless of how any of these specific models takes shape, teachers quickly begin to realize tangible pathways between creativity and learning, specifically in relation to language and literacy. The youth participants almost always have a hand in shaping their respective learning environments by writing original stories, reading comics by their peers, speaking to others about characters and plots, and listening to feedback from instructors and friends. It is not a coincidence that the New York State Standards in English Arts (New York State Department of Education, 1996) demand high-quality reading, writing, listening, and speaking. In line with the theories of John Dewey and writings of Maxine Greene, these educators have discovered ways to engage the youths in authentic literacy practices, despite many of the students having been labeled as "low performers." As a consequence, CBP expanded, first as an after-school initiative, with 33 comic book clubs in New York City. That number expanded to 67 two years later and over 500 comic book clubs nationwide.

It is not a coincidence that CBP was born in an after-school setting. There is a unique paradox inherent in out-of-school-time learning that has allowed for creative projects like CBP and many others to thrive (Bitz, 2006, 2008a). In most after-school settings, learning is mandatory, but attendance is voluntary. Therefore, after-school educators have had to unearth ways of supporting academic and social development while enticing youths to participate. The young comic book creators want their commas and semicolons to be correct because the comic books are *theirs*—the comics represent their ideas, identities, fears, and dreams for the future. Even for those students who never exhibited any prior interest in comics, CBP became a forum for self-expression and creative exploration.

Right from the outset, the issues that students chose to explore in their comics were difficult ones, ranging from gang violence to abusive relationships to teen pregnancy (Bitz, 2004a, 2004b). Because the comics were created after school hours, the range of acceptable themes was expanded to encompass the daily experiences of the youths at home and in their neighborhoods. Even first- and second-grade participants presented tough issues to readers through their comics: drug abuse, smoking, and gambling, to name a few. I argue that it is better to enable young people to explore such issues through their art and writing than to censor them as inappropriate for school discussion. This is not to say that random violence or curse words should be fair game in a student comic book. The most successful comic book clubs incorporate a discussion about the intended audience for the comics and the boundaries of acceptable content for that audience. I suggest approaching the issue of difficult content by asking, "If your little brother or sister were reading your comic book, what would you want them to see?" Or, "If your comic is all blood and guts, how many bookstores will put it on the shelf and sell it?" I delve more into the issue of content in Chapter 2.

STUDENT COMIC BOOK SELECTION

Regardless of moral or message, student comic books include plenty of action. A prime example is this chapter's selected comic book, titled *Elemental Revenge*—a classic superhero tale created by a group of middle schoolers in the Bronx. These boys assigned specific roles to the members of their relatively large group: Some were responsible for writing the story, others for drawing the scenes; one became a color specialist, and another became a rather skilled, albeit begrudged, proofreader. As we can tell from their cover design, featuring a robotic villain and an embattled superhero, this comic book is about good versus evil. The young artists and writers clearly took cues from popular comics and movies based on comic books in which a young, innocent boy discovers his special powers at the very moment of the earth's demise at the hands of a malicious criminal. Such characters and story lines are at the core of the comics canon, and these middle school boys were not immune to the allure of the superhero ethos.

The story begins on Planet Xerega, a giant red orb backed by a Swiss-cheese moon. I believe the name Xerega to be one of the best I have ever heard for a comic book planet; I could only smile upon learning that the boys had fashioned the name from Zerega Avenue, around the corner of their school. In the beginning of the comic, the boys make good use of a common element in comics design called a "thumbnail," essentially a box within a box. Their thumbnails feature a shocked male figure stuttering, "Wha is th-th that?" and "Wh-who are you?" Of course, from a literacy perspective, this would have been a perfect time to discuss sentence punctuation; questions always end with question marks, even on Planet Xerega. In any case, the last two panels of the first page exemplify the relationship between comic book panels and movie camera shots. The penultimate panel is a close-up on the hero's horrified face, hair afire and eyes and necklace glowing yellow with rage. The last panel is a pullback that encompasses exploding asteroids amid a giant "kaboom." Despite the big explosions, these young designers remind us that comics are all about the details. The last panel subtly features a small blue pod with a shadow of a figure inside. Perhaps our hero is still alive.

The boys move from the fictional Planet Xerega to real-life Planet Earth, represented by the two burning towers of the World Trade Center. Along with plumes of smoke and burning windows, the boys draw a simple diagonal line through the buildings, an omen of the impending collapse illustrated in the second panel. Taking a step back from this comic book created in 2006, these boys were 6, 7, and 8 years old during the terrorist attacks of

Figure Set 1. Devaughn Testman, Reinaldo Lassalles, Alcides Lopez, Pierre Castillio, Christopher Lopez, Demitrius Garcia, Nathaniel Singleton, Johnny Moore, and Ishrishad Clark (sixth–eighth grade), MS 203/East Side House Settlement, New York City

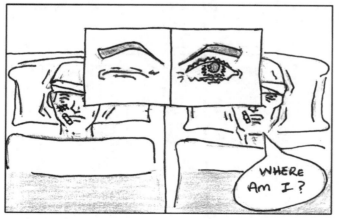

9/11. They experienced the shock of every other New Yorker that day, and they were subject to the same barrage of repetitive images on television and the Internet. In my opinion, it is a powerful opportunity for a child to employ creative writing and art as a synthesis of such a traumatic event. If CBP has accomplished nothing else over the past years, at least it gave these seven boys, and a number of other New York City children, a chance to make sense out of something so unimaginable.

Throughout this comic book, the group makes use of "word art"—the visual design of text to enhance the meaning of the words. They vary their fonts and point sizes, but they also illustrate some key words. On the first page, for example, they construct the word *boom* with big block letters backed by a spiral of smoke. The written text accompanied by the visual imagery of both words and art make for a dramatic introduction to the narrative—Planet Xerega is clearly in danger. The boys also make interesting use of captions and word balloons. In the opening, they create a caption—"Planet Xerega"—but instead of a typical caption block, they add a feature of word balloons to point to the red planet (as opposed to the moon in the background). The characters proceed to speak in word balloons, but then the action ramps up; the creators elect to forego the frames so that the words stand out, like "NOOOOO!!!" near the close of the first page. These middle schoolers demonstrate the flexibility of the comics medium—characters do not have to speak in word balloons, and captions do not have to appear in rectangular boxes. This freedom can be liberating for students and teachers alike.

To read the full-length, color version of this comic book, visit www.ComicBookProject.org/wcmk.htm

CLASSROOM APPLICATION

The end product of this chapter's featured comic book can be a bit overwhelming in light of the character development, plot twists, uses of color, and varied angles. Yet the comic book did not begin with all those literary and artistic elements; it began with the boys discussing comic books—their favorite comics and movies based on comics, characters they admire, artistic styles they appreciate, and why certain artistic styles intrigue them. They spoke and listened to each other before they wrote or drew anything, and in doing so they came to an understanding of how they might work together. They also quickly understood and embraced the skills that each group member would contribute to the process. Taking the time to discuss and brainstorm allowed for a productive team approach to creating the comic book before the creative process ever began.

Activity:

What Is a Comic Book?

Goal:

To introduce the comic book genre and engage students in deconstructing the medium for themselves.

Handout:

An age-appropriate comic book. See the Classroom Resources feature at the end of each chapter for ideas.

Procedure:

Have students read aloud or act out one or more pages of the story, with different students taking the roles of different characters. Students can even build a small set based on the images of the comic book.

Thought Questions/Discussion Ideas:

1. What are the key elements of a comic book?
   (Visual art, words, characters, stories, action, drama)
2. What would the comic book be without art? What would it be without written text?
   (Without art the comic book would be much like a movie script, with just basic dialogue and scene descriptions. Without written text the comic book would read like a story in pictures, but would not make much sense to the reader.)
3. What do you like most about this comic book? What would you change if you could?

Extra Activities:

1. Find a comic book of a completely different type. For example, an American comic book versus a Japanese one, or a modern graphic novel versus a classic comic book. (See the resources below for suggestions.) Explore the similarities and differences.
2. Translate one page of a comic book into either a movie script or a paragraph-based story. Be mindful of all the details as well as the intended sequence of the narrative. And be creative!

CLASSROOM RESOURCES

To build your classroom library, good resources for age-appropriate comics are

1. http://library.buffalo.edu/libraries/asl/guides/graphicnovels
2. http://www.ala.org/yalsa/ggnt

For the exercise in this chapter, the following books make for good examples of the comics medium.

Elementary school level:

Reynolds, R., & Numberman, N. (2009). *Joey Fly, private eye in creepy crawly time*. New York: Holt.
Smith, J. (2005). *Bone*. New York: Scholastic.

Middle school level:

Abadzis, N. (2007). *Laika*. New York: First Second.
Carey, M. (2007). *Re-gifters*. New York: Minx.

High school level:

Kubo, T. (2004). *Bleach*. New York: Viz.
Wheeler, S. (1998). *Too Much Coffee Man's guide for the perplexed*. Milwaukie, OR: Dark Horse.

CHAPTER 2

Scaffolding for Reading

For as hard as educators work to set all the blocks for literacy—phonemic awareness, word recognition, sequencing, story grammars—the purpose of all this is to transform children into independent readers, writers, and communicators. Every textbook devoted to literacy education at least mentions "scaffolding" (Bruner, 1986). Teachers learn strategies that scaffold learning in order to affect the "zone of proximal development," or "the distance between the actual developmental level as determined by independent problem solving and the level of potential development as determined through problem solving under adult guidance or in collaboration with more capable peers" (Vygotsky, 1978, p. 84). Scaffolding for young readers can take many forms. Informal scaffolding involves asking pertinent questions about texts: *Why does the furry character not want to taste the green eggs and ham?* Scaffolding can also be more formal. In order to help students make inferences about a story, for example, teachers can take a macro-cloze approach where students fill in a missing sentence based on the text and their personal experiences (Yuill & Oakhill, 1991). For example: *John went to the store, hoping it was still open.* (*Fill in a sentence.*) *He told himself he would have to come back first thing in the morning.*

SKILLS OF SEQUENCING

In building a scaffold for classroom reading, sequencing becomes one of the most important skills for comprehension and fluency. Most of us take sequencing for granted when we read—the order of events is logical as the author guides us with language, grammar, and sentence structure. For example, Henry James (1986) wrote in *The Portrait of a Lady*, "The old gentleman at the tea-table, who had come from America thirty years before, had brought with him, at the top of his baggage, his American physiognomy" (p. 61). Even with the inserted phrases and clauses, a plethora of commas, and the difficult word *physiognomy* (the relationship between appearance and character), we know the sequence of events: The man came from America 30 years ago and is now sitting at the tea table. Yet for a struggling reader who cannot wade through the verbiage or the vocabulary, the sequence is lost. Therefore, young readers need explicit strategies for the metacognitive skill of sequencing (Eilers & Pinkley, 2006).

Comics are exactly that—detailed sequencing road maps. Putting sequencing into the larger context of reading, Stadler and Ward (2005) present a continuum of narrative progress in early childhood: labeling, listing, connecting, sequencing, and narrating. Arguably the largest leap in this continuum is that between connecting and sequencing. A young reader or storyteller may be able to connect items in a list or themes in a story, but to place narrative elements into a logical sequence requires a good deal of critical thinking. The skills of sequencing go beyond recognizing "first, next, and last." A student has to understand (1) why one event comes before another, (2) the consequences of that sequence, and (3) the effects of that consequence on the rest of the sequence. Only then can a young reader move on to narrative, the end of the continuum.

By design, comics put sequencing into a visible, tangible context. It should be noted that comics do not simplify sequencing. In fact, the order of events in many comic book stories is rather complex; readers have to make a number of inferences about the characters' actions and intentions. However, comics do make the abstract concept of sequencing more concrete than in a paragraph story or chapter book. This is achieved through the construct of panels discussed in Chapter 1. Each panel frames a portion of the narrative's sequence. The reader is clear not only what comes first, next, and last but also why and how those things happen. Figure 2.1 is a good example. In the first panel, a man from above calls out to a boy below. In the second panel, the man—without speaking—dangles a rope ladder. The boy wrestles with a decision in the next two panels: climb the ladder or stay put? We learn of boy's decision as we see him struggling up the ladder at precarious heights. Is the man good or evil? The hand reaching out in the last panel indicates that he aims to help the boy.

The sequence of panels in a comic book is not always consistent—readers have to stay on their cognitive "toes" in order to follow the logic of the storyline. For example, in Figure 2.2, a continuation of the story from Figure 2.1, we no longer see the boy; the illustration shows the man alone on a rooftop. The reader must decide what happened to the boy. Did he fall off the ladder? Did he decide to go back down? Rather, the author changes the point of view by putting us in the boy's shoes—what he sees is what

Figure 2.1. Excerpted with permission from *Wireman* (2007), by Sue Stauffacher, Wireman Comics

**Figure 2.2. Excerpted with permission from *Wireman* (2007),
by Sue Stauffacher, Wireman Comics**

we see. Such knotty sequences are frequent in comics, and they encourage readers to think critically about the author's intentions and nonlinear flow of the storyline.

Creative Panel Construction

Comic book authors often employ creative panel structure, allowing for changes of pace within the progress of the storyline. The creator of Figures 2.1 and 2.2, for example, varies the panel sizes and then overlaps the panels to move the reader along in the story. Figure 2.3, by a group of elementary school students in New York City, is another prime example. The top two panels represent a confrontation between a bully in the first panel and a victim in the second. The separation of frames is emblematic of a standard comic book sequence. However, the ellipsis at the end of the second panel connects to the third panel in which the young authors use triangular enclosures to accelerate the action of the story. In each triangle, the reader witnesses the rapid unfolding of the conflict as the victim gets her revenge with an antibullying "bomb." One can imagine the difference in pacing had the authors chosen to separate these triangles across multiple panels on one or more pages of the comic book—the story would get bogged down. However, the authors were able to find a creative way of maintaining the sequence while adjusting for the quickened timing of events. The effect for the reader is one of excitement as the events of the story transpire in a reduced physical space.

Figure 2.3. Derek Crothers, Angely Flete, Chelsea Flete, Jarlene Gonzalez, Geomaris Martinez, Elhadji Thiam, Michelle Tineo, and Marcus Ortiz (second–sixth grade), PS 161/Harlem Dowling, New York City

Manga: Reading in a New Sequence

Manga is the Japanese term for comic books, and the Japanese style of comics has become extremely popular worldwide—a subject that I wrote about in *Manga High* (Bitz, 2009a). Manga sales in the United States generated more than $220 million in 2007, and about 1,468 titles were estimated to have been released that year and even more in 2008 (Reid, 2007). Like American-style comics, manga is sequential artistic-written narrative, constructed of panels, and driven by captions and word balloons. Many manga series are connected to animated cartoons, or *anime*, fostering ever more interest in the whimsical characters and stories that account for most manga. The genre is distinctly representative of Japanese culture and society. Brent Wilson (1988, 1999) demonstrated strong connections between manga and the personal identities of Japanese youths. When he asked Japanese children to create sequential narratives, they instinctively created manga—sequential narratives driven by uniquely whimsical characters and stories.

Manga may represent Japanese identity, but children in the societies of the United States, Europe, and other Western regions have embraced this comics form with exuberance. Teachers unfamiliar with manga may be extremely confused by observing students reading these comics; the books appear upside down. In fact, almost all manga translated from Japanese begin with a stop sign and the words "Stop! This book reads right to left. Flip the book over to begin the story." Because Japanese reads from right to left, most manga translated into English also follow this "backward" sequence. Although there are some American publishers who adapt their manga to Western left-to-right sequencing, most manga fans crave the authentic texts from Japan, and that entails rethinking the sequence. (See Figure 2.4 from a popular manga series as an example.) This may be a risky prospect for some educators. Cary (2004), for example, questions the use of right-to-left manga in educational settings because this format "muddies the reading waters" (p. 68). He asks: "Why have students reading right to left when English is read left to right? Why take a chance on even slightly disorienting students while we're working so hard to get them comfortable with the conventions of English reading?" (p. 68).

While manga may present new challenges in sequencing, it is important to engage children in authentic literature (Simons & Ammon, 1989; Tunnel & Jacobs, 1989). Young manga fans readily discern the differences between Japanese manga and "Ameri-manga." It would be a shame to discourage young readers from the books that they so readily embrace in lieu of versions more convenient for classroom instruction. Children pursue manga

Figure 2.4. Excerpted from *Bleach* (2001), by Tite Kubo, copyrighted by Viz Media

series originating from Japan not for the sake of sequencing, or any other skill touted by teachers, but for the sake of narrative; they identify with manga characters and become entrenched in the ongoing stories. To take these books away from children because they do not fit a standard model of literacy is a disservice. In fact, the practice of reading and writing manga from right to left forces students to critically think about sequencing, rather than simply taking the order of panels as a given.

STORY GRAMMARS AND STORYBOARDS

Regardless of whether children read and write American-style comics or manga, the storyboard structure of the medium is conducive to reinforcing story grammars, or schemes. Literacy theory tells us that children establish cognitive schema—that is, mental representations—of story constructs when they read a story or hear one read aloud. A mystery story, for example, typically requires the reader (and often a sly detective) to put clues together to solve a crime. Once children have been introduced to this construct, they mentally map the structure as the story unfolds. Fitzgerald (1989) summarized it this way: "[Children] use a sort of structural outline of the major story categories in their minds to make predictions and hypotheses about forthcoming information" (p. 19). Yet because different children have varied cognitive abilities, imaginations, and tastes in literature, their concepts of story grammars are not so set in stone. Therefore, teachers use a variety of techniques to support a wider array of story grammars, ranging from graphic organizers to story maps. A graphic organizer, for example, asks students to make sense of story elements by placing characters, setting, and other aspects of the story in a flowchart or diagram. A story map asks students to consider the most important elements of the story: Where and when does the story take place? Who are the most important characters? What is the main character trying to achieve? How does he or she achieve that goal?

The comic book storyboard structure offers a detailed combination of graphic organizer and story map. Students who struggle with the seemingly endless waves of words in a paragraph-based story can rely on the storyboard as a visual and textual guide to the most important elements of the story, including the sequence. We can imagine a student's thought process, represented by italics, while mapping a page of a comic book, using the first page of this chapter's student comic book selection. **Where and when does the story take place?** *The first panel shows a city street. The word "bank" is obvious, and there are some dollar bills. So the story probably takes place outside a bank, maybe during a bank robbery because of the police car in the second panel.* **Who are the most important characters?** *One character appears in all the panels—the one with black hair and triangular chin. He must be the main character.* **What is the main character trying to achieve?** *Well, every time the other characters do something bad, like rob a bank or steal a car, he is always there trying to tell them to think about what they are doing.*

As discussed in Chapter 1, the process of negotiating the text and visual imagery in a comic book for, say, a fourth grader is very much akin to how a kindergartner might "read" a picture book. Along with understanding the words, the reader must demonstrate "visual literacy"—making meaning from pictures, designs, and other images. For some reason, however, in American culture allowing pictures as a narrative construct is permissible for our youngest readers, but we systematically expunge the pictures from literature as children grow older. We expect school-age children to dissociate visual imagery from written texts, thereby stifling an important intelligence and ignoring the fact that our world, especially with increasing technological advancement, is a visual one. As Kellner (1998) wrote: "Education today needs to foster a variety of literacies to empower students and to make education relevant to the demands of the present and future" (p. 103). The increasing demand for a workforce and citizenry that is comfortable with multiple literacies, as opposed to one factory model of literacy, is at least one argument for why comics could have a place in an English language arts classroom.

READING COMICS AS LITERATURE

If comics do become part of the reading curriculum, teachers need to consider how they will be introduced, discussed, and analyzed, just as they would any other piece of literature. One approach is to present classic works in comics form, akin to the Classic Comics series, which began in the 1940s and then became Classics Illustrated to disassociate it from the comics medium. Over the decades, the series transformed *Moby Dick*, *Huckleberry Finn*, and many other novels into simple black-and-white comics. Although Classics Illustrated ceased production in the early 1970s, the model is pervasive today. For example, now one can buy *Shakespeare's "Hamlet": The Manga Edition* (Sexton & Pantoja, 2008) and *Comic Book Shakespeare: Macbeth* (Timber Frame, 2003), the latter available from the Royal Shakespeare Company.

Although the "classics comics" model might be the most direct connection to literature already rooted in the English language arts curriculum, I do not believe that this is the best way to introduce comics in the English language arts curriculum. Most of these books seem to undermine the original works as well as the comics medium; also, there is a temptation for students to use them like Cliffs Notes. Rather, select quality comics and treat them as literature: What are the themes? How do the characters evolve? What devices and techniques does the author use? What do the characters' actions say about their beliefs and moral standings? In this manner, comics become integrated into the very concept of literature, and students expand their palates for different literary forms and structures. Of course, there are many connections to be made between comics (e.g., *Maus*) and the accepted canon of literature (e.g., *Diary of Anne Frank*). Just as Odysseus has his defining flaws in the *Odyssey*, so does Batman in *The Dark Knight*. Carter (2007) thoroughly explores such connections between comics and classic novels.

LESSONS FROM THE COMIC BOOK PROJECT

One can imagine the challenges that school teachers might face in asking their students to create comic books during class. Limited time, as always, is an issue. In an English language arts classroom, the teacher would need to make time for visual art and design: sketching, drawing, inking, coloring, and much more. Conversely, in a visual arts setting, the teacher would need to accommodate writing and everything it entails—spelling, grammar, punctuation, story structure, and much more. Moreover, school and district administrators would need to support a creative approach to literacy building; parents would need to understand how the process of making comic books could help their children learn; students would have to want to participate in that process; and community partners would need to assist the project by supporting the culminating exhibits and publications. And, of course, all this would need to transpire within the culture of standardized testing and the many hours of test preparation that it entails.

How has the CBP overcome these challenges? Let's fly from New York to Cleveland . . . where administrator buy-in and interdepartmental collaboration allowed for the project to thrive during the school day. It was the Department of Arts Education at the Cleveland Metropolitan School District that took the lead. Department administrators introduced CBP to district art teachers and measured their interest in the concept. Over 45 teachers volunteered. In order to focus on the literacy components of the project, the art teachers agreed to partner with language arts teachers at their respective schools. The art teachers also voted on a theme for the project—conflict resolution. The Cleveland schools had been experiencing a spike in violence, and the teachers wanted students to contemplate peaceful problem solving via their original comic books. After a daylong workshop that I conducted with the teachers to launch the project, the Cleveland implementation of CBP was under way.

The teachers took a variety of different approaches to creating the comics. Some teachers decided to have students plan and write their stories in English class and accomplish the drawing, layout, and coloring in art class. In these cases, the teachers coordinated their efforts throughout the entire process. They developed a schedule that would accommodate other planned activities in the visual arts and language arts curricula, including the Ohio State Proficiency Tests. While this partnership model allowed for an interdisciplinary approach to creating the comics, it also raised some challenges. For example, one school made the students responsible for carrying their planned stories from English class to art class and back again. Invariably, a number of students misplaced their stories and had to re-create what they had drafted. In another school, the designated English teacher went on maternity leave in the middle of the year; her overwhelmed replacement was reluctant to take on the extra responsibility of CBP.

In other schools, the art teacher accomplished the entire process in art class—including the writing piece—while the language arts teacher acted as a consultant of sorts. Some of the language arts teachers helped correct spelling and grammar errors while others worked with individual students who were struggling with their storylines. This model put the art teachers in charge of the direction of the project, but it also added the pressure of ensuring high-quality literacy practices in a classroom typically devoted to creative art making. Many of the art teachers welcomed the challenge. Sherri Pittard at the Newton D. Baker School of Arts, for example, regularly incorporated writing activities into her art classes, so CBP was a natural fit. She asked students to not only write about their characters but also speak to the class about what they were planning and to provide constructive feedback to peers about strengths and weaknesses of the proposed comics. The artistic aspect of creating the comics became embedded into a broader approach to creativity that involved academic, social, and interpersonal skills.

Throughout the process, the issues of sequencing discussed earlier in this chapter were readily observed. In planning the panels of the comic books, students were required to consider how one panel reflected on the previous panel as well as how it would affect the panel to come next. One student remarked that creating the comic book was like putting together a puzzle. In fact, he took the initiative of cutting out the panels from his planning pages so that he could move them around as he saw fit. He enjoyed the kinesthetic technique of picking up a panel from his desk and moving it to another spot. In another school, the teacher had students write out their entire stories in paragraph form, then simply number the sentences of the story to represent the sequence of panels for the comic book. In yet another case, the students acted out each step in the sequence of their comics. They had a good time with the spontaneous drama productions while coming to an understanding of where their plans for sequencing needed some revising. For instance, a group of sixth-grade girls had sequenced two full pages of their comic as an argument between two characters. When they acted these pages out in front of the class, it quickly became clear that the monotony of the argument did nothing to advance the sequence of the story.

By the end of the first page, the class dissolved into laughter, and the group of girls went back to the drawing board.

Given the theme of conflict resolution, the Cleveland teachers and students also engaged in considerable thought about story grammars. Many of the boys associated conflict resolution with fighting, and their first drafts featured long fight sequences. But the goal of this project was in part to help students think about a variety of situations that involve conflict and how to appropriately resolve those situations. I observed one class that spent several sessions discussing conflict resolution before ever picking up a pencil. The teacher believed that it was crucial for the students to get to the heart of why people fail to communicate and resort to violence. Hence, the students discussed some very deep and challenging issues: poverty, race, inequality, civil rights. Eventually those discussions led to original stories that morphed into comics. Not coincidentally, the comics reflected many of the same themes that the students had discussed as a group. In other words, their story grammars expanded beyond the conventional categories that one might predict, including action, humor, horror, and romance. In creating their comics, these students and many others in Cleveland began to find their own voices in the learning process by developing and defining original stories about themselves, their schools, and the surrounding communities.

Over the course of the school year, the Cleveland students and teachers went from story sequences to drafted manuscripts to penciled sketches to fully developed comics. Many of the students were extremely excited with what they had created, and many of the teachers were proud of what their students had accomplished through the process. The Cleveland Public Library agreed to exhibit select comics from each school; the students, along with their parents, teachers, and community members, were invited to the library for an opening reception and celebration. At the event, students were invited to present their comics by introducing the characters and events of the story. I witnessed a number of students walk their parents through every panel of the comics, narrating each detail of the story. One mother said with amazement to her son, "I never imagined you could do something like this. I just never imagined."

The Cleveland project concluded with the collection of student comic books for the citywide publication titled *Peace in Our Schools*. The months-long process of developing characters, drafting manuscripts, and designing comic books had come to a close. The project evaluation—surveys, interviews, and site observation—indicated that the initiative had been a success. However, as teachers began to enter the room, something was clearly amiss. Many teachers were in tears. Some consoled their colleagues, while others sat at tables with their heads down. As I soon learned, the district had announced widespread layoffs; the art teachers knew they would be hit hardest. For some of the teachers, these comic books were a final testament to everything that they had accomplished during the year.

Despite this inauspicious conclusion to the first foray of CBP outside New York City, many of the Cleveland teachers who returned to their schools the following year remained committed to CBP. With each passing year, new teachers signed on, and veteran teachers helped newcomers to understand the goals and expected outcomes of the project. In this way, the teachers themselves eventually adapted the model to the needs of their own classrooms and learning goals. The result was an in-school model of comic-booking that influenced other school districts nationwide. The project also affected many students for years to come, as one participant wrote me in an email:

> Hello! This is Marchanna, co-creator of "One Thing to Another" along with Kayla and Danielle. (We were the students from Scranton Elementary in Cleveland.) It's been over 2 years now—I'm now 13—and I think I neglected to tell you how thankful I am that you founded the Comic Book Project. It's such a great way for students to interact and discover and build up their artistic talent. And also, if it wasn't for this project, I would not be so fond of manga to this day, gotten *much* better at drawing, or even had start my own manga series! I was wondering if you are running the Comic Book Project in any Hope Academies this following school year? I would LOVE to participate in this project once more! Thank you for taking time to read this, Mr. Bitz! I look forward to hearing from you. With All Due Respect, Marchanna

Marchanna neglected to mention her improvement in writing, as made evident by the note she sent. She properly introduced herself and told her story. She followed up with a question, and then a closing. Her use of punctuation was masterful: she hyphenated *co-creator*, used quotation marks around the title of her story, included opening and closing parentheses around the next sentence, and then demonstrated proper use of an em-dash. Whether or not Marchanna becomes a writer to make her living, she certainly developed some solid career skills. And who knows? Maybe her new manga series will be on the shelves of bookstores one day.

STUDENT COMIC BOOK SELECTION

The selected student comic book from Cleveland highlights the reading scaffold necessary for us to understand such a complex piece of narrative. The skill of reading for sequence is required right at the outset. Reading left to right, the text of the first panel asks, "Why do you want to take his money?" This does not make much sense until we see the caption, which the author intended to be read first: "One day this man was going to the bank so he could get some money. Then this man came up behind him." In this first panel, we are introduced to the Master Mind and an unnamed character up to no good. We know this from the boy's words, but also notice his right eyebrow—an indication of "sneakiness" if there ever was one. Taking in our schema from the first panel and moving to the next, we now know how to sequence our reading: caption first, then word balloons.

Panels 2, 3, and 4 form their own sequence. Panel 2 features a boy—different from the one in the opening—stealing a car. Panel 3 shows another boy about to smoke a cigarette. And Panel 4 shows a violent fight in the making. In each of these panels, the main character hovers above, always trying to convince the boys to do what is right. The first page ends with our "hero" screaming with rage: "No one is listening to me!!" Now we have a sense for why his face is battered—the consciences of these characters are seriously injured.

At this point in the story, the reader forms a schema about what will happen next: Either the boys will get away with their crimes, or they will get in trouble. As the comic makes clear, the latter transpires. The mugger is in jail. The car thief gets arrested. The smoker must heed an ominous portent from the main character: "Now look at you. You let them get to you! You will die now." Readers connect these consequences with the original actions from the page before; a logical story grammar unfolds as we work through the text and visual imagery.

It is also important to examine a comic book such as this from a literary perspective. Even though the author is only in eighth grade, he employs creative devices of a mature comic book creator. For example, only the head of the main character appears throughout—why? Given the artistic skill demonstrated, the student certainly could have drawn a body for the character. Yet the student aims to reinforce that the main character is, in fact, not a person but the consciences of the other characters. Therefore, the character's head floats around the panels, trying to make his point to the other characters: listen to your conscience. The last panel of the penultimate

**Figure Set 2. Jose Angel Vargas (eighth grade),
Joseph M. Gallagher School, Cleveland**

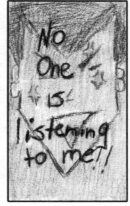

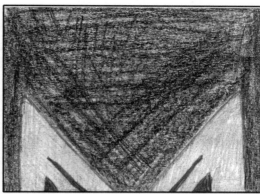
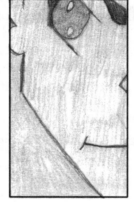

page highlights this nicely; the character's hair is replaced by a brain, and a thought balloon extends from his neck. In the end, the boys get what they deserve with the warning: "What goes @ comes @!!" Retribution is a theme that many great authors, from Dante to Joseph Heller, have explored, and this student author is making his literary contribution.

To read the full-length, color version of this comic book, visit www. ComicBookProject.org/wcmk.htm.

CLASSROOM APPLICATION

Retelling is a useful skill for developing reading comprehension, specifically for reinforcing story grammars and structures. Many teachers encourage writing projects as a conduit for retelling something that students read (Hansen, 2004). Creating a comic book is an equally advantageous method of retelling, and that is the focus of this activity.

Activity:

Scaffolding for Reading Through Art and Writing

Goal:

To engage children in reading synthesis through the creation of a mini–comic book.

Handout:

A story that students have read or are currently reading in class, or use the story starter below, which students can extend.

> The neighborhood seemed to burst with color as Leslie hurried down Washington Avenue just past Prospect Park. The Jamaican curry shop—green, red, and yellow—sent a cloud of smoke from the grill onto the bustling sidewalk. Leslie spotted Jay, as always dressed in his Giants gear, still brimming from the Superbowl upset. "Hello," she said breathlessly. "Is Eric back?" "Nope."
>   Leslie's smile turned to a frown. She closed her eyes, trying to hold back the tears she knew would come. She had waited 3 months, though it seemed like 10 years, since Eric had left. Each week his letters promised that he would make

it back to the neighborhood soon. "Seems like he lied," Leslie said to no one.

Suddenly a rush of gray dust swirled in a torrent of wind. The door of the curry shop slammed closed with the force of the gust. People darted everywhere, clasping their groceries to their bodies or shielding their eyes with briefcases. Jay's prized Giants cap flew high into the air, but he didn't move an inch. With his eyes bulging wide and his hair on end, Jay peered into the chaos. He gasped, "Is it him?"

Out of the settling dust emerged a blinding blue light that encompassed everything in sight—the people, stores, buses. The wind abruptly ceased as if it too were consumed by the overpowering light. Leslie squinted into the brightness to follow Jay's gaze. Twenty feet up the sidewalk, a dark figure was slowly emerging. A shimmering aura surrounded the figure. And then he appeared. Eric was back!

Procedure:

Have students retell the story in three to five panels of a comic book. Working in pairs or individually, the students should first write a plan for what they will include in each panel; students can sketch some ideas as well. (One suggestion is to turn each paragraph into a panel.) Then students can design the panels as a retelling of the story, keeping in mind important details from the story and inferences that they have made about the characters. Next, have students continue the story in both paragraph and comic book forms. Have students present what they created to the class.

Thought Questions/Discussion Ideas:

1. How is the retelling of the story through the comic book form different from the story in sentence form?
   (The comic book form relies on visual images to show some of the details while the sentence form relies exclusively on words.)
2. Is it OK if different students interpreted the story differently, leading to different comic books?
   (Of course it is! That is the beauty of art and writing.)
3. What clues did the author give you to help you retell the story?
   (Character descriptions, adjectives, metaphors, and so on.)

CLASSROOM RESOURCES

Books for linking comics with traditional literature and bringing comics into the English language arts classroom:

Carter, J. (Ed.). (2007). *Building literacy connections with graphic novels: Page by page, panel by panel.* Urbana, IL: National Council of Teachers of English.

Frey, N., & Fisher, D. (Eds.). (2008). *Teaching visual literacy: Using comic books, graphic novels, anime, cartoons, and more to develop comprehension and thinking skills.* Thousand Oaks, CA: Corwin Press.

Wolk, D. (2008). *Reading comics: How graphic novels work and what they mean.* New York: Da Capo.

Websites for comics in the classroom:

http://www.teachingcomics.org
http://teachinggraphicnovels.blogspot.com
http://wardmancomics.googlepages.com

Comics that lend themselves to literary discussion:

Elementary school level:

Aragone, S. (2009). *Groo: Hell on earth.* Milwaukie, OR: Dark Horse.
Claremont, C., Cockrum, D., & Byrne, J. (2006). *Essential X-Men.* New York: Marvel.

Middle school level:

Van den Bogaert, H. W., & O'Connor, G. (2006). *Journey into Mohawk Country.* New York: First Second.
Yang, G. L. (2006). *American-born Chinese.* New York: First Second.

High school level:

Satrapi, P. (2004). *Persepolis: The story of a childhood.* New York: Knopf.
Spiegelman, A. (2003). *The complete Maus.* New York: Penguin.

CHAPTER 3

Scaffolding for Writing

C hapters 1 and 2 of this book have focused on the role that comics can play in scaffolding for reading. However, there are also extraordinary applications for comics as scaffolding for *writing*. Writing instruction has been the focus of CBP since its inception. Surprisingly few researchers have focused on the connection between comics creation and conventional writing instruction. Of note, Morrison, Bryan, and Chilcoat (2002) advocated student-generated comic books as a culminating activity at the close of a unit. Wright and Sherman (1999) presented comic strip development as a writing activity. Perhaps the reason for the relative disconnection between comics and writing is that teachers are so much more focused on reading, and even speaking, than on writing in the classroom (Gunning, 2006; National Commission on Writing, 2006). Emergent writing activities typically take a backseat to emergent reading, when, in fact, young children practice writing "skills" through scribbling before they begin the process of reading (Sheridan, 1997; Sulzby, 1992; Sulzby, Barnhart, & Hieshima, 1989). The challenge that many teachers face in encouraging children to write is that the realm of writing goes well beyond forming letters of the alphabet. Writing is a way for students to re-create and represent the surrounding world as well as the world inside—their ideas, thoughts, and identities.

In many ways, writing is an art, as is teaching writing (Calkins, 1994). Not coincidentally, pre-writing begins with drawing pictures. Engaging young elementary schoolers in meaning making through self-generated pictures is a good activity, but a better activity for early literacy development would be sequential picture making as a reinforcement of the elements of narrative. This is exactly what the first and second graders at PS 180 and PS 182 in Harlem accomplished through CBP in partnership with Say Yes to Education, a nonprofit organization based at Teachers College, Columbia University. The children, most of them English language learners, created one- or two-page comic books about a hero in their lives. While many of their comics incorporated elements of text-based writing, their stories were driven by the pictures that they had created. Hence, students who were struggling with spelling and sentence construction were still able to fully participate in the writing activity. Furthermore, I as a reader needed the students' oral narration to fully understand what the mini-comics were about, thereby reinforcing the important skills of speaking and listening.

Unfortunately, just as we discourage older students from visual imagery in their reading texts, we quickly force students past first grade to write without drawing. We institute "correct" and admonish "incorrect" ways of writing; the creative aspects of invented spelling and free-form composition morph into the undeniably boring routines of dictation, penmanship, and other linear skills. And then we wonder why students come to dislike writing. Creating comics enables students to retain creativity in the writing process while reinforcing all the basic writing skills that teachers aim to instill: planning, rehearsing, composing, revising, and editing.

In the pre-writing processes of planning and rehearsing, for instance, young comics creators imagine how their characters will look, what they will experience, and how they will act. Since these characters and topics extend from the children rather than a teacher, the students are much more likely to write (Graves, 1975). As far as composing, students must draft a story, first by planning the overall plot and then by outlining each panel of the comic. By focusing on a panel-by-panel composition, students overcome the challenge of not having enough to write about, a common problem for elementary schoolers (Scardamalia & Bereiter, 1986). Those compositional drafts become the bases for the actual comics, enabling students to focus on revising and editing before they produce a final result.

Moreover, the thousands of students involved in CBP have demonstrated that discussions and activities based on the typically dry subjects of grammar, spelling, and punctuation come to life in the context of creating comic books. A series of workbook exercises on the proper use of commas can be mind numbing, but reinforcing comma usage within the context of a superhero's dialogue becomes much more palatable for most students. In one particular classroom of fourth graders in New Jersey, the students had discovered the power of the exclamation point, especially in their action sequences. As the tension increased in the scenes, the students gleefully added more exclamation points. One group of students established the climax—the final blow to the villain—with nine exclamation points. This became the perfect opportunity for the teacher to ask the students to put down their pencils and engage in a discussion about ending punctuation. She explained how the overuse of exclamation points diminishes the effect for readers, and she used the students' comic book drafts as examples. The students immediately understood their punctuation gaffe, and they had a good laugh in trying to re-create the reading—rather, screaming—of a sentence with nine exclamation points.

THE WRITING SCAFFOLD

The writing scaffold used by CBP is supported by essential parts of the comic book–making process: character development, story development, dialogue crafting, and caption building for the purposes of drafting the comic book, followed by revising, inking, and coloring in order to present and publish the comic books. In the drafting stage, character and story development are most pertinent to the pre-writing and planning stages; dialogue crafting and caption building relate directly to the skills of composing and writing mechanics. A look into each of these four "quadrants" elucidates just how applicable comics are to the range of writing skills introduced in the English language arts classroom.

Character Development

Comics—whether developed by Frank Miller, Chris Ware, CLAMP, or a third grader from the Bronx—are driven by characters. Iconic characters have fueled the growth of the comic book industry since its inception, and some of those characters (e.g., Superman and Batman), have survived many decades of powerful nemeses, making them truly "super." Just like professional comic book designers, children who create comic books want their characters to have a "hook," something that makes the characters stand out. For example, the fifth-grade boy in New York City who created the image shown in Figure 3.1 developed an environmental superhero. The character has a trashcan for a head and an emblem of "SG" on his chest, for "Super Garoy." This hero flies over the Elmhurst neighborhood of Queens and battles sludge monsters and other dastardly villains bent on destroying the city with their refusal to reduce, reuse, and recycle.

However, many of the students involved in CBP do not create comic books about superheroes (Bitz, 2004b). Their comic books more often feature everyday people, children and adults who overcome real-life issues: peer pressure, drug abuse, gang recruitment. While these characters are fictionalized, they are often drawn from the students' personal experiences. As teachers know, many youth face such challenges on a daily basis.

For example, the female character shown in Figure 3.2, created by a

Figure 3.1. Fernando Acevado (fifth grade), PS 89Q, New York City

fifth-grade boy from Cleveland, had an argument with her best friend over whether to pool their money for a movie. She wants to spend their money, but the friend wants to save his share. The girl obstinately sticks to her position, convinced that her friend is cheating her. But then the girl happens upon the friend on the street corner and sees him putting his money into the bag of a homeless person sleeping on the corner. The homeless person turns out to be the boy's aunt. It is not until the girl puts herself in the position of her friend that she recognizes her own error in judgment and says, "I never thought of that. I'm gonna tell him I'm sorry right now!!"

While almost all students who create characters for comics will do some

Figure 3.2. Angelo Crenshaw (fifth grade), Miles School, Cleveland

drawing to capture visual depictions, the written descriptions of the characters are just as important. Students write the characters' names, ages, and hometowns at the outset, but then they write in more depth about the backgrounds of the characters. Those students who rely more on their linguistic than visual-spatial intelligences describe how the characters will appear in the comic instead of sketching images. The image shown in Figure 3.3, by a sixth-grade boy in New York City, is an example of a combination of written and artistic descriptions of the characters. This student created the written description first, but he had a mental image of how these characters would appear. His writing helped him to hone that image so that his sketch could accurately match what was in his mind.

As made evident by the character development shown in Figure 3.3, students are already planning the structures of their stories as they brainstorm the nature of their characters. These characters do not live in a vacuum; they exist for the purpose of conveying the intended storyline soon to be developed. In this sense, character development and plot development are not distinct pursuits. Children contemplate their stories as the characters develop on the page in art and writing, and many times the character plans change as new ideas for a story come to light. In one case, a student planned four characters for her story but whittled the number down to three as she thought about how the characters would interact. In another case, the students worked together as a group to develop a "character continuum" (Barton & Sawyer, 2003), a technique that they had learned from their reading class. This tool for character analysis demonstrated how their main characters would change over the course of their comic book. In other words, even though the group had yet to plan what would actually happen

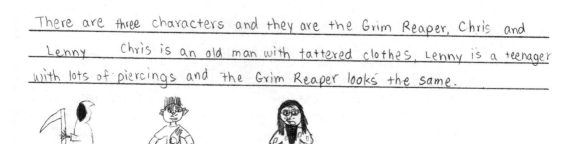

There are three characters and they are the Grim Reaper, Chris and Lenny   Chris is an old man with tattered clothes, Lenny is a teenager with lots of piercings and the Grim Reaper looks the same.

Figure 3.3. Tim Zhang (sixth grade), MS 216, New York City

in the story, they knew what they wanted their characters to learn and how they would grow.

Story Development

With the characters in place, students begin to compose their stories with a combination of written text and sketched art. This is a drafting stage—students should not be concerned with spelling, grammar, or punctuation at this point, nor should they spend any significant time on drawing detailed images. The concept of a first draft can be troubling for students who have never before engaged in a lengthy literary project. From the writing perspective, many students have trouble separating their ideas from how those ideas are represented on the page. Calkins (1986) noted about elementary schoolers: "They continually interrupt themselves to worry about spelling, to reread, and to fret. This 'stuttering in writing' leads to tangled syntax and destroys fluency" (p. 16). A similar stumbling block presents itself with sketching, as opposed to complete artistic designs, which eventually appear in the final comic books. Especially for artistically developed students, the concept of creating a simple design can be frustrating, unless children are taught how to sketch (Bartlet, 2005). Maintaining sketchbooks alongside journals (or within journals) is a good way to keep the creative ideas flowing while encouraging the dual processes of writing and drawing.

The process of story development varies among classrooms and even among individual students in a classroom. As mentioned in Chapter 2, some educators—usually English language arts teachers—have their students write out the entire story in paragraph form, then number the sentences in order to represent how the paragraph-based story will transform into the panels of a comic book. This is a good approach for building compositional skills, but it immediately sidetracks the visual conception and artwork for the comic book. Other teachers—often art teachers—ask students to sketch their comics in storyboard form to portray the sequence and layout. Doing so allows for a strong visual concept but makes the writing component secondary. The most comprehensive approach is for students to develop both aspects of their comics, written and artistic, simultaneously. Doing so fosters multiple skills and intelligences. Furthermore, this multifaceted approach allows for unique collaborative opportunities between self-described artists and writers in a classroom. One note about such collaborations, however: It is important that every student take ownership of the writing and drawing in a comic, even if they have designated roles in the process. It would be a shame for the artists in a classroom to never get the writing opportunities afforded by comic book composition; the same goes for the writers and the potential for artistic development.

Dialogue Crafting

Whether in the compositional stages of first and second drafts or within the panels of the actual comics, much of the writing that appears in a comic book is through dialogue—the actual speech delivered from a character's mouth. As discussed in Chapter 1, dialogue is usually framed within a word balloon, which allows the writer to imagine exactly what the character is saying and how the words will be spoken. This unique aspect of writing in comics makes writing less abstract than in the paragraph formation of a conventional story. In writing a comic book, students can imagine the character's words, speak aloud that dialogue with appropriate tone and inflection, then write the words on the page. Contrary to the common impulse of students to draw the word balloon first and stuff their writing into that space, students should write the dialogue and then design the word balloon around the text. This procedure enables students to concentrate on the written words and then reflect on how the frame of the word balloon enhances the intended meaning.

There are a variety of word balloons in the tradition of comic books, representing declarations, thoughts, exclamations, questions, and more. A discussion of these frames can be helpful, but students often invent their own word balloons depending on what they are aiming to convey with the dialogue. The work shown in Figure 3.4, by a tenth-grader in Tucson, represents just how creative students can get with their dialogue and word balloons. Here the evil little character shouts his demand with big block letters—a good example of "word art." However, his words are framed

Figure 3.4.
Hans Sebastian Rivera
(tenth grade),
Pueblo Magnet High School/
Pima Community College
Upward Bound, Tucson

by a standard word balloon without any remarkable features. Is the effect diminished? Not quite—the character himself is surrounded by a jagged yellow frame, which embodies the speaker rather than what is spoken. An example such as this represents the limitless possibilities of text and imagery in the hands of a creative risk-taker in the classroom.

Perhaps the most pressing concern for educators related to crafting dialogue is whether slang and dialect ought to be allowed. Many teachers demand proper English whenever students pick up a pencil to write. In the context of a comic book, however, such a stipulation is counterproductive. In every case, the students' characters are in part representative of the students themselves; to force the characters to speak "properly" is to defeat the entire purpose of engaging youths in the process of creating comics. Rather, the topic of slang and dialect should be discussed with students— using talk fosters students' understanding of audience, appropriateness, and literature in general (Strickland, 1988). Furthermore, slang is part of the comics vernacular. For instance, an investigator on a crime scene in *Watchmen* (Moore & Gibbons, 1986) says, "Well, looks like someone broke in by bustin' this door down" (p. 2). The informal language helps to set the scene and establishes the essence of the character. In this manner, students should have the opportunity to explore different elements of language within the dialogue-crafting process. As this process continues, teachers can ask frequent and pointed questions about what students have written: *How does this dialogue represent the character? Will readers understand what you are trying to say? Do varied dialects help readers differentiate between the characters in the comic book?*

Caption Building

One way to facilitate the understanding of differences between slang and proper English is to encourage students to incorporate some captions into the comics. Since captions extend from the outside voice of a narrator, they naturally lend themselves to conventional English rather than slang— unless, of course, students intend for the narration to take on a certain voice. Regardless, captions help guide the reader through the comic, and they can help students control the pacing of the storyline. Like dialogue, captions are usually framed, oftentimes in a box at the top or bottom of a panel. Yet unlike dialogue, captions allow readers to peer inside characters, to get a sense of what characters are thinking or feeling. Whereas dialogue establishes a connection between the characters and the reader, captions facilitate a connection between the author and the reader. The use of dialogue and captions allows writers an extraordinary amount of flexibility, deciding whether to speak through characters, narration, or a combination of both. Add the visual imagery to this mix, and the scaffolding for literacy through comics development becomes all the stronger.

FINISHING THE PRODUCT: REVISING, INKING, AND COLORING

Revising

As with any writing project, the first draft of a comic book is not the finished product. A good amount of revising is necessary for students to hone their writing and art. Because of this, it is crucial that students draft their comics in pencil with little hand pressure so that they can erase mistakes. Also, once a student has drawn the outlines for original panels, teachers can photocopy the panel layouts so that the student can produce several drafts without having to redraw the boxes. The revision process varies across classrooms, but there should be some opportunities for a teacher to meet with a student (or group of students working on the same comic) and review mechanics, character development, and plot structure. The revising stage is also an excellent opportunity for peer review. As a teacher meets with one group of students, the other groups can review various comics in process and provide written comments on a separate sheet of paper. This model enables students to get as much feedback as possible before they begin to revise their work. A teacher could even establish an in-class "revision conference" or workshop, ensuring that every comic book is set for a quality revision. As Graves (1983) notes, "Revisions that children make as a result of the conference can be at a much higher level than those made when the child is working and reading alone" (p. 153).

Revising can be an overwhelming prospect for young comic book makers, especially given the need to revise writing *and* art. A good approach is to focus on one element of the work at a time (Spandel, 2001). For example, a revision schedule might first begin with story structure followed by character development and design. With these larger issues in place, the students can focus on smaller details, beginning with writing mechanics and sentence structure in conjunction with page layouts and panel designs. Finally, a focus on grammar, spelling, and punctuation completes the revision process. An overemphasis on these smaller details at the outset could stifle a student's creativity and overall interest in the project. Revising takes time, so students should become invested in their stories, fostering a *need* to correct grammar, spelling, and punctuation.

Inking and Coloring

Once the comic books are drafted and revised in pencil, some schools opt to "ink" the pencil drawings and text with very thin black markers. (Students have also used black ballpoint pens quite successfully.) Kneaded rubber erasers work well for removing pencil lines after inking. It is important to note that inking is a very time-consuming and precise process, akin to editing in a movie cutting room. However, the result of inking is a more readable, professional-looking product. Inking is an art unto itself; certain inking techniques can dramatically change the tone of a comic book. In a good resource for artistically advanced students, Martin (1997) thoroughly explored inking and provided examples of the same image inked in different ways. Many teachers forego inking altogether, usually because of time constraints. A unit plan should allow at least three class sessions for inking if it is to be accomplished effectively.

After inking, students may add color. Chapter 8 describes desktop publishing technologies for color production, but a simple way to start is with colored pencils, which allow for corrections and superior control. Crayons are too clumsy; markers can bleed through the paper. A good process is to color one character at a time throughout the entire comic book so that the characters look consistent. Remind students to keep color out of the dialogue bubbles (unless there is a good reason for coloring them).

Inking and coloring are not mere design elements of comics. These techniques wholly support the written narrative. Take color, for example. A scary story would be undermined by brightly colored backgrounds and rich hues. A light story, in contrast, would be enhanced by these elements. Professional comic book creators think very carefully about the inking and coloring of their comics—in fact, the largest publishers have artists who specialize in these areas. Students can model this attention to visual detail by photocopying their penciled pages and experimenting with different colors and inking techniques. Of course, this too takes time, but the end result is almost certainly worth the effort.

LESSONS FROM THE COMIC BOOK PROJECT

In CBP, we discovered that an exercise was needed to facilitate the drafting and revising processes—a bridge between the opening activities focused on the creative elements of comic booking and the actual comic books that students would produce. The Manuscript Starter became that link—a drafting tool that allowed students to write about and sketch their characters, develop a plot, and plan their comic books by jotting and sketching ideas for each panel. In reality, the Manuscript Starter was simply blank paper with some prompts to elicit student writing:

Who are your characters?
What are their names?
Where do they come from?

Then students were encouraged to sketch their characters, with the reminder: "Remember . . . it's not about drawing skills; it's about creativity." Before jumping into the pages and panels of the comics, the Manuscript Starter asked students to write at least three sentences for their plot: beginning, middle, and end. With these planning elements in place, the students were better equipped to write and design their comics.

How each CBP site took the journey from draft to published comics varied based on the needs of each school, community, and classroom. One site planned to create an entire comic book–publishing company with production designers and a business team. Another site wanted to institute a comic book club because the art program had been cut from the school; the afterschool initiative would be the only artistic activity that the students would experience. Yet another site wanted to institute separate comic book clubs for the boys and girls, enabling them to concentrate on their art and writing rather than each other.

Some students were clustering their ideas about "community" by listing the positive and negative things that they had witnessed in their neighborhoods, then circling the items that they would incorporate into their comics and crossing out the others. Other students were using pencils and spiral notebooks to journal ideas and possible storylines, which they were to present to each other during the next club session. Many of the sites had students working in groups, and I observed a number of shared writing responsibilities. In one case, three girls had drawn three characters—likenesses of themselves—and then began writing conversations between the characters. The girls were silent during this process, but they smirked and smiled at each other as they read what their partners had written. By the time the club session ended, the girls had drafted the basis of their comic book: Three young females in the park find a bottle of magic perfume that attracts boys, but they decide to spend their time cleaning up the park instead.

Most project sites also exhibited art making early on in the process. The majority of students seemed unabashed about drawing, which was surprising to many of the teachers and me. "They get it," one instructor said to me. "They're focusing on being creative and not worrying too much how it all looks. They're into the stories." As with the writing, the artistic endeavors took a variety of forms. Some students concentrated on character sketches; others enjoyed drawing their homes or schools. Two boys collaborated on the design of a car. After failing to get the wheels just right, they went to the computer in the corner of the room and downloaded a picture of a Ford Mustang as their model. Another pair of boys shared the design of the main character in their comic book—one boy drew the body, and the other created the face. They drew at the same time, coordinating their arms, hands, and pencils over the page.

The most successful classrooms in terms of the revision process were those in which teachers modeled what they expected, oftentimes including a revision checklist. They used examples from the student drafts to demonstrate clarity or solid sentence structure, always making sure to find an opportunity to praise every student, even if the draft required extensive revisions. To demonstrate the importance of a good conclusion, one teacher had students present their comic book in front of the class but stop short of the conclusion. He then asked the rest of the class to predict the conclusion, allowing the group in front of the class to realize that the comic needed more details to guide the readers. This same teacher had students question each other about their comics. Each student devised questions for every other student, which helped everyone collect a plethora of ideas for improving their comics.

STUDENT COMIC BOOK SELECTION

The comic book selection from Baltimore is titled *Be a Friend*, and it focuses on the theme of community building within a school. This comic book represents the fundamental differences between creative development and artistic skill; most sixth-graders could draw what appears in this comic book. Like many "indie" comics creators, this girl relies on the witticism and emotion of the story rather than superior artistry. In short, this piece is a model as to how an engaging comic book can be very simply drawn and designed.

We can trace the writing scaffold through this story. Beginning with character development, the student introduces a main character named Wolf. He is new to the school and desperate to make friends. Wolf's problem, however, is that he does not look like the other students. At first glance, he appears to be an alligator. One detail informs us otherwise—

Figure Set 3. Miriam Harris (sixth grade), Stadium School, Baltimore

in the background of the first panel is a girl's bathroom, boy's bathroom, and . . . alas, Wolf is a dinosaur. With this introduction, the student focuses on story development. Wolf, looking as different as he does, becomes a victim of bullying. As one would expect, Wolf is distraught. The second panel demonstrates how simple lines and shapes can convey a bounty of meaning. Wolf's downcast eyes, raised eyebrows, hunched shoulders, and drooping mouth indicate heightened sadness. The story develops with the introduction of a girl named Nici, who befriends Wolf; the two become fast friends and help each other through a difficult situation with the bullies.

The inking and colors of this comic book demonstrate the effectiveness of these tools in supporting narrative. The inking highlights the dialogue and word balloons, but the author also inks particular character features to make them stand out—including Wolf's tears on the first page and the steam rising from his angry expression on the third page. The color choices add to the dramatic effect. For example, on the third page the student chooses a red background to represent Wolf's ire and a blue background for Nici's sadness. The student also uses warm colors to represent positive emotion, such as the yellow and red in the second panel of the second page: "Best Friends." The varied colors of the final panel highlight the importance of the comic's overall message: "Take the lead! Make a friend."

To read the full-length, color version of this comic book, visit www. ComicBookProject.org/wcmk.htm

CLASSROOM APPLICATION

As discussed throughout this chapter, interesting characters are the foundation of good comic books, and character development is a core element of the creative-writing process. The participants in CBP often develop their characters before anything else, including the plot, panel layouts, and artwork. The following activity is helpful for students to brainstorm characters while honing important writing skills.

Activity:

Superheroes and Villains

Goal:

To focus on character development as a collaborative project.

Handout:

Some blank paper and pencils.

Procedure:

Part I:

Begin with a class discussion about the biggest problems in the
world that students would want to change (e.g., poverty, violence,
hunger). List the students' suggestions on the board. Then place
the students into groups of two, three, or four. Ask each group to
develop a superhero that would combat one of the issues on the
board. Each group should produce (a) a drawing of the superhero,
(b) a name for the superhero, (c) a slogan for the superhero, (d)
three complete sentences to describe the superhero, and (e) five
adjectives that represent the superhero's strengths.

Part II:

Have each group pass its completed superhero from Part I to another group. Ask the groups to now design a villain—the nemesis
of the superhero that was passed to them. Each group should
produce (a) a drawing of the villain, (b) a name for the villain, (c)
a slogan for the villain, (d) three complete sentences to describe
the villain, and (e) five representative adjectives (antonyms of the
adjectives from the superhero).

Part III:

Once the superheroes and villains are complete, have a group
present its superhero followed by a presentation from another
group for that hero's nemesis. Each group should present an
original superhero and villain.

Thought Questions/Discussion Ideas:

1. Why is it important to plan your comic book before you start
   drawing?
   (Planning gives you an outline of what you want to draw.
   Without the plan, you might have to start over in the middle
   of your comic book.)
2. Why are interesting characters important for the success of a
   comic book?

(Good characters carry the story. Also, comic book creators aim to publish multiple issues in a series based on the same characters. Customers won't buy new releases if they don't like the characters.)

3. What was challenging about developing superheroes and villains from the activity?
(Ask if students found it difficult to go from drawing to writing or vice versa. Did the students assign themselves certain roles in the process?)

Extra Activities:

1. Plan and then create a two-panel mini–comic book based on a book that you have recently read.
2. Extend the three-sentence descriptions of the superheroes and villains into a paragraph-based story.
3. Develop sidekicks for the superheroes and villains. For each sidekick, include a drawing, name, written description, slogan, and appropriate adjectives.

CLASSROOM RESOURCES

Resources for writing and drawing comics:

Abel, J., & Madden, M. (2008). *Drawing words and writing pictures.* New York: First Second.

McCloud, S. (2006). *Making comics: Storytelling secrets of comics, manga, and graphic novels.* New York: HarperCollins.

Sturm, J., Frederick-Frost, A., & Arnold, A. (2009). *Adventures in cartooning.* New York: First Second.

Comics that support the writing scaffold in terms of character development, story development, caption building, and the other elements of comics design:

Elementary school level:

Hall, M. C., & C. E. Richards. (2006). *King Arthur and the Knights of the Round Table.* Mankato, MN: Stone Arch.

Holm, J. L., & Holm, M. (2005). *Babymouse: Our hero.* New York: Random House.

Middle school level:

Gownley, J. (2009). *Amelia rules! The whole world's crazy.* New York: Simon & Schuster.

Vaughan, B. K., & Henrichon, N. (2006). *Pride of Baghdad.* New York: DC Comics.

High school level:

Abel, J., Soria, G., & Pleece, W. (2008). *Life sucks.* New York: First Second.

Fujisawa, Y. (2008). *Metro survive.* Fremont, CA: DGN.

CHAPTER 4

Collaborating for Success

R eading and writing are usually thought of as solitary practices. When we think about "curling up with a good book" or "writing the great American novel," other people generally do not enter the picture. Yet as I have indicated throughout this book, creating comics is oftentimes a collaborative process. This is true not only of classroom comics but also of professional publishing in the largest comics publishing houses. A comics publication from Marvel, DC, or Dark Horse Comics involves pencilers, inkers, colorists, letterers, cover designers, art editors, layout specialists, writers, copyeditors, and proofreaders—not to mention all the other people responsible for getting the comic book to the public: marketers, salespeople, accountants, webmasters, and more. The finished publication, therefore, is the result of efforts by many people. All these people have artistic and literary skills relative to their specific employment, but they must also demonstrate strong interpersonal, organizational, and time-management skills. If one person does not meet expectations, the entire team and resulting comic book suffer. Therefore, to refer to Stan Lee's *Daredevil* or Mike Mignola's *Hellboy* is a bit misleading. However, without these original creators—without their creative *ideas*—these comics would not exist, and neither would the jobs for all the writers, artists, editors, and marketing associates.

As with professionals in a commercial publishing house, children enter the classroom with a range of skills and intelligences. Those who excel at writing often become responsible for the manuscript and editing of dialogue, captions, and storylines. Artistically developed students typically draw characters and design the backgrounds of panels. Children with clear penmanship are usually recruited to write the text in the finished comics, transferring the words from the draft to the finished product. And just as DC Comics, Dark Horse Comics, or any other major publishing company needs to bring its products to an audience, students with strong interpersonal skills invite family members and friends to exhibits and presentations via printed invitations, email campaigns, and word of mouth. The students aim to create as strong a "buzz" about their comic book exhibit, as Marvel Comics does with an international movie release.

Children work together on the very seed of a comic book by brainstorming and discussing the core elements of a story: *Who are the main characters? What happens to them in the comic? How can we make it original?* The concept among children often originates with the team. I have never seen an individual student conceive an idea for a comic book so that other students could develop the product. Club schedules change, stories evolve in the editing process, supplies run short at a school—many factors affect the creation of comics in class. In the end, however, if a group of children begin the process, they are all equally responsible for completing it. It is not only teachers who emphasize this dogma; students can be their own toughest critics.

This is not to say that all student collaborations ensue smoothly. Children often have a difficult time composing their own ideas for others, and vociferous arguments about any number of issues related to the comics—characters, dialogue, cover designs—are common. Successful (and peaceful) solutions are most evident when a teacher has a system in place for conflict resolution. One teacher who initiated a group comic book project posted her system next to the whiteboard and had children recite the points before every class:

1. Let each member of the group speak while others listen.
2. Write down at least three possible solutions to any problem.
3. Vote on the solution, and choose the one with the most votes.

If a group of students approached the teacher with an unresolved conflict, she made sure that the students had followed this process first. Problems among group members were almost always successfully settled by proceeding through the steps. However, four members of a particular five-person team continually vetoed the ideas of the fifth student. The teacher subsequently added a fourth rule: Every team member must have at least one idea represented on every page of the comic book.

Where teachers have not instituted a concrete set of class rules for group work, students themselves are responsible for the negotiation process; a variety of problem-solving methods have evolved (Bitz, 2006). At one site, each of the group members assigned himself a different character in the comic book. Each student was always responsible for how his character appeared, talked, and behaved. If another student was opposed to something in the story, the character, rather than the student, put forth the opposition and worked it into the storyline. At another school, students threw dice to decide how the story would progress. Each of the three group members developed an idea for the next part of the story and picked a number; then the group rolled the dice until one of the selected numbers surfaced—a random but fair way of giving group members equal influence in the decision-making process. The excerpt below from an observation of three seventh-graders illustrates how the collaborative process can transpire:

> *John:* Let's have the villain come down from Mars and take over the city.
> *Frank:* No, from a planet that nobody's ever heard of.
> *Lucy:* But I just said the villain was a cop. He's bad and does crime and stuff, remember?
> *John:* But I drew this cool guy, with all these arms. See?
> *Frank:* I know, let's have the bad cop turn into this monster whenever he's gonna do something bad.
> *John:* Yeah!
> *Lucy:* Um, OK. But I can't draw that thing.
> *John:* No, you draw him when he's the cop, and I'll draw him when he turns into the monster.
> *Lucy:* OK, yeah.

KEYS TO SUCCESSFUL COLLABORATIONS

There is a strong precedence for collaborative writing in a classroom setting. Guided writing—modeled after guided reading—establishes a workshop setting where students and teachers write, reflect on writing, and write some more (Collins, 1998). Through mini-lessons followed by writing time, guided writing workshops give students the opportunity to practice specific writing techniques such as developing an effective story ending or varying sentence patterns. Because such workshops put writing into social as well as cognitive realms, teachers work to maintain healthy group dynamics and minimize problems such as teasing and unconstructive criticism (Lensmire, 1994). A workshop necessitates that all the writing pieces are in progress. None is better than the other, and all require feedback and encouragement from workshop participants.

Finding Time: The Solution of Mini-Lessons

The most crucial aspect of collaborative writing projects is that of time, that is, giving students enough time to become thoroughly invested in the writing process (Calkins, 1994). As any author can attest, writing is a time-consuming pursuit that cannot be conveniently stuffed into a 38-minute class period or a few homework assignments. Children need time to not only complete writing assignments but also reflect on what they have written, make changes, and share with others, all in the effort to produce high-quality work. Of course, time is a luxury that most teachers cannot afford, given all the required content and skills that need to be covered over the course of a year. But the most successful teachers make time for writing and embed those skills and content areas into daily writing activities. The more children write, whether individually or in groups, the better they become at writing. Teachers who learn how to engage children in writing during science, social studies, and even math lessons maximize the opportunities for students to become excellent writers.

Everything that pertains to collaborative writing in a conventional setting applies to group writing in a comic book. Rather than being presented with the overwhelming task of writing a complete comic book, students excel with a number of mini-lessons related to the overall project. These mini-lessons can be presented at the start of the process, or they can evolve depending on the needs of the particular writers in a group. An example of a mini-lesson might be to ask the members of a group of students to each write a sentence about a character in the comic. Then students can compare and discuss what they have written, eventually combining their sentences to form complete character descriptions. A mini-lesson such as this enables every student to have some independent writing practice while contributing to the efforts of the entire group. This is good literacy practice, especially if children have defined roles for themselves that do not concern writing—artists, inkers, or cover designers. Artistically inclined students need as much exposure to writing as anyone, and likely more so if they have chosen for themselves nonliterary responsibilities in the course of developing a comic book.

Creating an Environment for Collaboration

Also important in the context of a comic book is establishing a supportive environment for group writing. Children have a range of writing skills; some will make many more errors in spelling and punctuation than others. Teasing causes struggling writers to become more self-conscious about their abilities; hence, it is crucial for strong writers to mentor those in the group who need additional support. Students can support each other through peer review as long as a process for corrections and revisions has been established. One strategy to institute such a process is through "interpersonal writing"—written conversations between students and teachers (Duffy, 1994). In the context of a collaborative comic book, students can take on the voices of their characters and conduct written conversations from one character to another. As students pass around the papers or notebooks where the conversations reside, students make note of corrections in spelling, grammar, punctuation, and writing mechanics without making another student feel insecure about what he or she has written. These conversations can be incorporated into the comic book and can even help drive the storyline.

As with any collaborative writing project, however, the ultimate key to success with creating comic books is providing enough time for students to write, revise, edit, discuss, and repeat the process several times over. The initial brainstorming and drafting process of a collective comic book might take less time than a paragraph-based story—students can rely on their panel sequences to write ideas without concerning themselves with transitional sentences and paragraph structures. However, after those initial phases, the group often takes much longer with a comic book than a conventional story because they have to consider how the words affect the visuals and vice versa. Even though the comic book writing style is simple, the process can be lengthy, especially if multiple opinions and personalities are involved. This is especially true of the revision process, as noted in Chapter 3. On the other hand, there are ways of maximizing the members of the group to facilitate a steady progression of writing. Once the initial plan is set, for example, each group member can be responsible for writing a page of the comic book, or students can take on different roles in the writing process, such as spell checker, punctuation reviewer, dialogue specialist, and caption developer.

COLLABORATIVE ART MAKING

Every educator would agree that all students must develop writing skills and participate in classroom writing activities. But how many educators would insist that every student build artistic skills and participate in drawing activities? Unfortunately, in many schools the arts are relegated to infrequent electives, and in difficult economic times the arts tend to disappear from school altogether. The idea that art making pertains only to skilled artists is a mentality fostered not only by some teachers, administrators, and parents; students themselves become very self-conscious about creating visual art (or music, dance, or drama) if they have not been identified as artistically "talented"—a charged and problematic word. The consequences of such thinking (and policy) affect not only children's creative abilities but their cognition as a whole. As Perkins (2008) noted, "The way in which we create a schema—like Piaget's set of hierarchical stages—to describe developing behaviors and abilities—that's science. The way in which we see beyond the schemas—that's art" (p. 12). We need to recognize the importance of both ways of thinking and foster them equally in youth (Efland, 2002; Eisner, 2002; Hetland, Winner, Veenema, & Sheridan, 2007).

Even though the comic book process in school might parallel that of a large publishing house, children do not write in school for the purpose of becoming professional authors—they write to communicate with others, share ideas, and reflect on personal experiences. Similarly, children do not create art in school to become the next Pablo Picasso or Jack Kirby—they draw for the same reasons that they write. They draw as a means of expression and creative exploration. They draw to explore new ideas and ways of thinking about and seeing the world. Those students who aim to further develop their art skills should be offered electives and extra classes, but every student should have the opportunity to make art not just occasionally but during the course of every school year beginning in kindergarten and on through the end of high school.

A comic book project demands art making often in settings where visual art rarely surfaces, such as English language arts classes and resource rooms. I argue that every student involved in the project should make some art, even if the bulk of some students' responsibilities rests in the literary realm. Collaborative art making is an excellent way to focus the artistic process on creativity rather than drawing skills. If students practice drawing characters, backgrounds, and other images as a team, they all contribute to art making in the drafting stages and eventually to the outcome of the finished comic book. A system of "guided art," much like guided reading or writing, helps to cultivate an inclusive atmosphere where all students can draw without fear of being compared to others or derided for something that they design. A teacher can present mini-lessons in art that anyone (including the teacher) can execute. One such lesson is to have students draw a facial expression with six or fewer lines. By limiting the number of lines, students are forced to rely on their creative skills rather than artistic abilities. Figure 4.1 shows a prime example by a fourth grader. Of course, the lesson could be extended to incorporate literacy building: Students could write three adjectives for their facial expression, then pass their paper to a partner, who writes antonyms for those words and draws a new facial expression.

Figure 4.1. Carlo Rodriquez (fourth grade), Hartford, CT

Workshopping the Artistic Process

Many of the same criteria for successful group writing practices apply to collaborative art making. A workshop setting enables students to revise, edit, discuss, and improve their drawings, with the understanding that their first drafts are exactly that, not finished products. Peer review can be extremely successful but only if students have worked on the interpersonal skills necessary for providing feedback and constructive criticism to fellow students. With practice, every student reviewer should be able to provide some element of praise and some advice for improvement for every drawing. This leads to a sense of "deliberative democratic evaluation," where every voice is valued in the evaluation process in line with a set of predetermined guiding principles (House & Howe, 2000). In this context, a student might say in reference to another student's work: "The hands on this villain are really great—the fingers look like the talons of an eagle. I think the drawing could be larger, though, so it looks more important in the panel."

But most important, once again, is the element of time. Collaborative art requires time for discussion and reflection—skipping these elements of the process defeats the workshop concept entirely. Most teachers likely have less time to devote to art making than they do for writing activities, but there are ways of building artistic activities into class time. For example, if students draw a panel of a comic book, their reflection of the drawing could be a written journal entry, oral discussion, or multimedia presentation, all of which hone reading, writing, speaking, and listening skills.

Good workshop models for collaborative art making in a comic book project can be adapted from a more common form of group art: murals. Many schools use murals as a way of building teamwork, organizational skills, community involvement, and, of course, creative art development (Densel, 2005; Gurney, 2008; Kirker, 2007; Merrill, 2008; Prokop, 2007).

Such projects require students to take on different roles in these large art pieces while contributing to the whole of the project. Students must work together for the project to be a success, and they must take into account different students' abilities and strengths within the art-making process. Furthermore, because these are public works, mural projects require students to communicate with not only each other but also other stakeholders in the outcome of the mural: teachers, parents, school administrators, school staff, and community members. Embedded into this, therefore, are many opportunities for honing writing skills. For example, students might write a mission statement or a fully developed proposal for the mural. They could write letters to community partners and local artists to solicit their support. They could write a press release to announce the opening of the mural. These and other ideas that have emerged through group mural design are readily adaptable to a collaborative comic book project.

Individuals and the Group

While collaboration is an important part of the overall learning experience, some students might be more successful working as individuals during particular points in the process. For example, a student artist might need the creative "space" to explore different designs without outside interference. Similarly, a student writer might want to sit alone in a corner for a while in order to craft a story with the right tone. Even when working in a group, students should have opportunities to develop their own ideas and techniques—again, as they would in a large professional publishing house. A teacher could institute "group" and "individual" work schedules, but a more authentic approach would be for the students themselves to decide when they need to come together and when some individual work needs to get done. Such an approach fosters high levels of communication and advanced social skills.

Of course, a teacher could implement a comic book project in which every student creates his or her own comic book from start to finish, including all the necessary elements of writing, designing, revising, inking, and coloring. There is something to be said for a student who can accomplish such a large task on his or her own. However, the most successful individual projects still allow for plenty of communication among students. After each step in the process, teachers have students share and comment on each other's work. They might rely on a workshop setting so that students who are working individually still have a network of peer support to share ideas or concerns about structure, narrative, and mechanics. No matter how the project unfolds—in groups or as individuals—it is crucial that every student have multiple opportunities to share and discuss what he or she created with the entire class and a community at large not just at the end of the comic book process but all along the way.

LESSONS FROM THE COMIC BOOK PROJECT

Numerous collaborative models have emerged from CBP. In Chicago, high schoolers in Chicago were "hired" as apprentices. Their charge was to create original comic books on a pressing community issue and then distribute the works to others in the community through presentations, exhibits, and publications. The students who signed on to the comic book apprenticeship were excited to be creative, help their communities, and receive a monetary stipend. However, none of them had any experience in creating a comic book.

This was quite a problem at the outset for the 25 high school students who composed the club at Fenger Academy High School. The two instructors hired to lead the club were experienced comic book artists, an assured asset. On the other hand, they had little experience working with youths, especially ones without strong artistic backgrounds. The instructors launched the first class with an introduction and presentation of the project with a focus on its goals and expectations. Then there were several moments of uncomfortable silence as the students, overwhelmed by the task before them, waited for guidance on how to proceed, and the instructors, overwhelmed by the students before them, realized that their own creative processes were intuitive rather than explicit. Having never taught or even explained how they themselves create comics, the instructors were at a loss about how to motivate the students to get started.

Two things resolved the problem. One I reported in *Manga High* (Bitz, 2009a): The Chicago students happened to see a publication of comics produced by a high school club in New York City. These works created by like-minded youths in another city turned out to be inspirational. The second factor that moved the students beyond their creative impasse was a simple statement by one of the students: "Why don't we form departments? Some of us can draw. Some of us want to write. Some of us want to work on computers. If we can put it all together, then we can make a comic book." I liken this statement to the starting gun of a race. Without any prodding from the instructors or me, the students quickly began to figure out who would participate in which department—writing, art, editing, and layout. After some brief negotiations between students, the desks screeched around the room and the departments were set. An immediate problem arose. What would the editing and layout departments do, since there was nothing as yet to edit or layout? The entire class decided that rather than departments, they needed distinct teams, each with a writer, artist, editor, and layout designer. All the members of a group would work together on every step of the process.

Observing the sudden rush of action, the instructors gave each other a shrug, and then began to move around the room, consulting with the various groups and lending ideas and support. This is exactly what the students needed. Foregoing their original plan to "teach" comic books in front of a silent class of students, the instructors became mentors. They helped the students reflect on ideas for their comics, and they introduced some basic concepts of design and drawing. As each group produced character sketches, the instructors provided suggestions for making the drawings better; their comments usually related to the proportion of body parts or incorporating interesting details into a design. They taught the students how to relax their hands while drawing and techniques for creating perspective. The students readily accepted these mini-lessons because the tasks were for the purpose of developing *their* comic books rather than comic books in general.

This model of collaboration that came to be in Chicago highlights the importance of flexibility in the classroom. The educators charged with leading the class had a preconceived notion of how the learning would occur. When that plan fell short, the class was at a standstill. This is a common experience for many new teachers—after hours of lesson planning and preparation, the plan seems to go awry in real time. But these educators had good instincts; when a student offered a collaborative solution and the rest of the class agreed, they facilitated the group effort and used their strengths as artists to bolster the students' creative output. They created a workshop setting in which students could freely share ideas and then revise their comics in light of feedback from peers and the professional artists themselves. Because of this, the students became much more confident about their individual skills. They also became extremely close friends, bound by a mutual newfound veneration for comics and the two artists who first introduced the medium to the class.

STUDENT COMIC BOOK SELECTION

The four girls who created this comic established their own process for how to work together. The girls took several sheets of blank paper. At the top of one sheet the students wrote "characters," on another sheet they wrote "story ideas," and on another "community issues." On each sheet, they wrote and drew snippets of ideas and storylines that might eventually make it into the comic book. Rather than keeping this self-initiated planning process to themselves, the students in this group excitedly shared their brainstorming method with the other groups, which readily adopted the simple but effective strategy. They deliberated on several important community issues, including crime, pollution, and the high cost of living. In the end, however, they decided to create a frank comic book about domestic violence.

With the theme set, the girls assigned roles for themselves: writer, artist, letterer, and editor. They decided on these positions relatively early on in the process, but they also agreed to consult with each other all along the way, from the beginning ideas to the finishing touches. One example of a decision that they made together was to draw the comic book by hand but write the text on a computer, print it out, and paste the words in the appropriate panels. This shared responsibility became all the more important when the girls elected to tell their story from the point of view of a woman writing in her diary; hence the title *Teenage Abuse/I Am*. "Teenage Abuse" represents the theme; "I Am" represents the diary as well as a mantra repeated throughout the comic book.

The authors choose to open the comic on a large portrait of the featured woman rather than a series of panels. As the woman introduces herself through her personal writing, the four girls who conceived the comic are also introducing themselves. The voice of the woman in her diary entries is their collaborative voice—her words are their words. The diary entry begins: "I am an African American woman who's willing to give to the needy children. I am an African American woman who doesn't like when children are homeless." This is a compassionate and caring woman; these are compassionate and caring students.

One of the most difficult decisions that the girls had to make was whether or not to portray physical violence in their comic book. The girls believed that a depiction of the man beating the woman would force readers to confront domestic violence rather than skirt the issue with metaphors. But they also recognized that showing a violent scene might limit their

Figure Set 4. Tamika Mack, Tashima McDonald, Ebony Wilson, and Tiffany Jones (tenth–eleventh grades), Fenger Academy High School, Chicago

I AM AN AFRICAN AMERICAN WOMAN WHO LOVES THE CHILDREN.

I AM AN AFRICAN AMERICAN WOMAN WHO CARES ABOUT HER EDUCATION.

I AM AN AFRICAN AMERICAN WOMAN WHO DOESN'T LIKE WHEN KIDS GOSSIP.

I AM AN AFRICAN AMERICAN WOMAN WHO WISHES ALL THE VIOLENCE WOULD STOP.

I AM AN AFRICAN AMERICAN WOMAN WHO WANTS THE WORLD TO BE FULL OF PEACE.

I AM AN AFRICAN AMERICAN WOMAN WHOSE BOYFRIEND BEATS HER.

I AM AN AFRICAN AMERICAN WOMAN WHOSE BOYFRIEND WON'T LET HER LEAVE.

I AM AN AFRICAN AMERICAN WOMAN WHO IS TIRED OF THE THINGS SHE HAS TO PUT UP WITH.

audience and reduce their chances for inclusion in the school art fair at the end of the year. Rather than making a hasty decision, the girls drafted the comic book with and without scenes of violence, shared the versions with peers and the instructors, and then made a decision among themselves. The last panel of the second page puts the woman in front of a mirror. As she looks at her reflection, so does the reader. Her black eye peers out at us. The image is much more harrowing than any display of bloody violence.

The final page of the comic shows the boyfriend continuing his abuse—but she has had enough. As the type size of the text gets larger, we can imagine the woman's, and students', voices getting louder. "I am an African American woman who wants to be FREE. I am an African American woman who has drawn THE LINE." In the very end, they make a point of underlining (by hand) for emphasis: "I will *NOT* be ABUSED!!" The girls who created this comic book may not have had much experience in comic book design, but they certainly exercised the medium as a powerful tool for social justice.

To read the full-length, color version of this comic book, visit www.ComicBookProject.org/wcmk.htm

CLASSROOM APPLICATION

Collaborations in the process of making a comic book vary across classrooms. Here is one creative method of collaborating that enables every student to be part of every step of the process. Also, at the end of this application, the class will have numerous "story starters" that can become full-length comic books.

Activity:

Comic Book Pass Around

Goal:

To foster group work in the context of formulating original comics.

Handout:

A blank piece of paper and pencil for every student.

Procedure:

Students are each going to create a small part of a character or storyline, then pass the paper to the next student, who will continue the character or storyline. Each stop of the paper should last only a few minutes so that the class moves quickly and completes a full character and story idea in a single session.

First, have every student draw a face at the top of his or her paper, then pass the paper to the next student. Next, have every student create a torso for the face before him or her, then pass. Next, create some legs for the character, then pass. Now name the character and pass. Next, write some dialogue for the character, then pass. Next, design a word balloon around the dialogue; pass. Now write a caption to accompany the character and the dialogue. Pass again, and flip the paper over. Now write a sentence to start a story about the character, then pass. Write another sentence to continue the story. As this process goes on, students will have each worked on the assets of every character and storyline going around the room. Once students get their original sheets of paper, which contained only a face at first, the students can present to the class how that face turned into a full-fledged character with a storyline.

Thought Questions/Discussion Ideas:

1. Did the finished character appear as you imagined when you first designed the face? Why or why not?
2. What other characters would you add to the story to make it into a comic book?
3. How does creating a comic book with everyone in the class differ from creating one as an individual or with a small group?

Extra Activities:

1. Use the story that began with the activity to create a comic book. Choose one of the characters and storylines that you like best.
2. Trade manuscripts of your comic book with a partner. Provide some suggestions about the story and point out any mistakes that you find in spelling, grammar, capitalization, or punctuation.
3. Trade manuscripts of your comic book with a partner. Sketch some ideas based on what you read, and give your sketches to your partner so that he or she can incorporate your ideas into his or her comic book.

CLASSROOM RESOURCES

Resources for collaborative learning:

Snodgrass, D. M., & Bevevino, M. M. (2000). *Collaborative learning in middle and secondary schools: Applications and assessments.* Larchmont, NY: Eye on Education.

Thousand, J. S., Villa, R. A., & Nevin, A. I. (Eds.). (2002). *Creativity and collaborative learning: The practical guide to empowering students, teachers, and families.* Baltimore: Brookes.

Udvari-Sulner, A., & Kluth, P. (2008). *Joyful learning: Active and collaborative learning in inclusive classrooms.* Thousand Oaks, CA: Corwin.

Comics created by collaborations of artists and writers:

Elementary school level:

Bullock, M., & Lawrence, J. (2006). *Lions, tigers and bears: Fear and pride.* Berkeley, CA: Image Comics.

Owen, E., & Elder, J. (2006). *Mail order Ninja.* New York: TokyoPop.

Middle school level:

Hunter, E., Jolley, D., & Barry, J. (2007). *Warriors: Warrior's refuge.* New York: TokyoPop.

Van Lente, F., & Dunlavey, R. (2006). *Action philosophers: Giant-sized thing.* New York: Evil Twin Comics.

High school level:

Foglio, P., & Foglio, K. (2006). *Girl genius: Agatha Heterodyne and the circus of dreams.* Seattle: Studio Foglio.

Henderson, J., & Salvaggio, T. (2006). *Psy-comm.* New York: TokyoPop.

CHAPTER 5

Teaching Comics, Learning Life

Comic books straddle a delicate line between fine art and commercial illustration. While most professionally published comic books are created as a literary pursuit and means of self-expression, those works are also (for the most part) created to be sold to a market. For children, of course, the literary pursuit and self-expression take precedence; most students are not creating comics for a profit. However, they are creating their comics to be consumed. Students expect that their comics will be read by at least classmates and family members, and possibly many more readers if they post their comics on the Internet, which many students do. (See Chapter 6 for more on publishing student comics.) A number of young comic book makers have created extended series of comics, producing numerous issues with recurring characters. Friends line up to get the next addition, literally hot off the presses of an overworked photocopier. One weary student informed me that he stayed up all night to finish the next installation of his series because his friends pestered him to such a degree for the comic book.

It would seem that the sharing of comics with an audience would stifle the willingness of children and adolescents to divulge personal feelings or ideas. Yet this is not the case. Most students create their comics with a heightened sense of self-identity if they know that their comics will be read by others. They aim to capitalize on the opportunity to say something about themselves or where they live. By putting their words into the mouths of comic book characters, students find a voice and, in turn, an outlet for self-expression. There is a strong precedence for self-expression and identity exploration through the comics medium; even comic strips represent something significant about their creators. Avid readers of *Peanuts* eventually learned that these lovable characters represented the personality traits of their creator, Charles Shulz: Charlie Brown, his insecurities; Schroeder, his dedication to his craft; and Snoopy, his belief in the limitless possibilities of creativity (Michaelis, 2007). A more contemporary example is the manga *Hayate, the Combat Butler* by Kenjiro Hata (2008). Here the indigent

16-year-old main character becomes a butler and, in doing so, becomes a vehicle for the author to explore issues of class.

It is similar with children—their comics are representative, directly or indirectly, of the students who spawn them. As with Shulz and *Peanuts* or Hata and *Hayate*, the transfer of identity is often masked by the fantastical characters in the comic. Figure 5.1 shows a selection from a comic book created by three fifth-grade girls in New York City. Their theme was "bullying backfires." Instead of presenting a typical bully and victim, these girls chose to present the causes and consequences of bullying through a resentful maple tree and a jealous apple tree. The trees frown and fuss over each other as the seasons change. The farmer and visiting school groups seem to favor one tree over another with each shift in the weather. To exemplify further, Figure 5.2—created by a large group of students from second through sixth grade—employs sand crabs in their comic book about bullying. The largest crab forces smaller crabs off the beach, his sharp claws clacking in their faces. Both these comics use characters to represent the thoughts, ideas, and identities of the children who created them, even if those characters sprout leaves or sport an exoskeleton.

**Figure 5.1.
Yi Wen Huang, Mindy Zou,
and Kelly Su (fifth grade),
PS 120/Flushing YMCA,
New York City**

Figure 5.2. Connie Cui, Steven Koh, John Li, Sophia Liu, Ayden Soto, Lhasangpo Yarnang, Liaysia Beebe, Shelby De La Cruz, Meng Zheng Gao, Angelica Jacobs, Jailene Leonardo, Kalae Mobley, Christopher Medavilla, and Amari Wilder (fourth–fifth grades), PS 134/Henry Street Settlement– Helping Horizon, New York City

In other cases, the characters in the comics are the students themselves; the voices of the characters are the direct words of the young authors and artists. Molly, the fifth-grade girl from Cleveland who drafted the story excerpt in Figure 5.3, lists herself first in the litany of characters. These characters use teamwork to save their school, which has been vandalized by "creeps." Another frequent approach by students is to put themselves in the comic book, only years later in life. The image in Figure 5.4, created by another fifth-grade girl from Cleveland, features the author as a main character but as a tall 18-year-old. The student imagines herself several years down the line and considers how she will deal with peer pressure at that time. The story has the male character, Flex, prodding the girls to buy and drink some beer. Riquita, the author, has to decide if she will not only participate but also continue to associate with this group of friends. In the end, one of the girls decides to drink the beer and gets very sick. All four of the characters, including Flex, recognize their transgression and agree to support each other in making good decisions in the future.

Regardless of whether students elect to feature themselves or fictional characters in their comics, the end result is a reflection of life experiences and expectations for the future. These personal identities surface in a variety of ways—from heroes and villains to the storefronts that appear in the background. Each pencil stroke and every word on the page extends from the student, a series of both small and big decisions that students

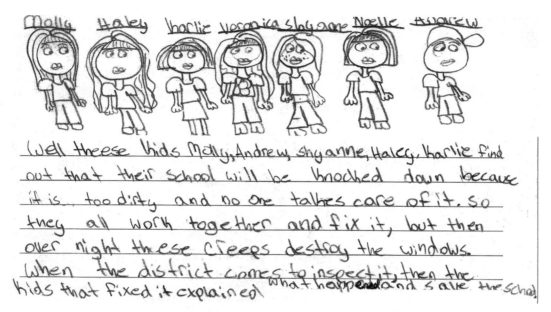

Well theese kids Molly, Andrew, Shyanne, Haley, Charlie find out that their school will be knocked down because it is too dirty and no one takes care of it. So they all work together and fix it, but then over night these creeps destroy the windows. When the district comes to inspect it, then the kids that fixed it explained what happened and save the school

Figure 5.3. Molly Medlik (fifth grade), Artemus Ward School, Cleveland

make while planning and designing their sequential artistic-written narratives. This can be said of all visual art, in fact, yet one unique element of the comics medium makes reflections on life all the more pertinent: the storyline. Self-portraits, landscape paintings, or marble sculptures

Flex is 18 and tall, Lenise is 17 and middle hight, Char is 19 and short, and Riquita is 18 and is tall. There are 4 characters in my comic book. Their names are Riquita, Lenise, Char and Flex.

Figure 5.4. Riquita Coston (fifth grade), Newton D. Baker School, Cleveland

provide insight into the artist who created those works. But comics put characters into situations via a storyline. Every time a comic book character makes a decision, the outcome is reflective of the author and the identity behind the work. For students, this is an opportunity to imagine themselves in difficult situations and consider the outcomes of their decisions. A fifth-grade girl thinking about the consequences of alcohol consumption later in her high school years is a good measure of this girl's identity now. It is also a valuable opportunity to prepare for some of life's most difficult decisions.

A teacher might aim to foster such self-reflection through journaling, poetry, and other traditional writing activities, which are, of course, valuable. But these pursuits are rooted in the first person. In a journal entry, for example, students expect to write about themselves, even though the teacher often says, "Write about anything." Poetry is more abstract, although still often oriented toward the first person. In contrast, only a handful of comics submitted to CBP have been written in the first person. Even those that are, as with the student example in Chapter 4, the "I" does not necessarily refer directly to the author. For some students, the distance from "I" and "me" can be empowering and no less reflective of the author who created the work.

THE FOUNDATIONS OF LEARNING

The need for young people, particularly at the middle school age, to explore their personal worlds alongside the world around them has been well documented by developmental and cognitive psychologists as well as educational theorists. A pioneer in art education, Victor Lowenfeld (1947) identified stages of artistic development; the "dawning realism" stage (ages 9–11) and the "pseudorealistic" stage (11–13) encompass the very essence of comics art as put forth by youths. The medium also enables children to embrace later stages of aesthetic development—"expressiveness," "style and form," and "autonomy"—by focusing on different stylistic approaches and considering how the resulting images reflect on an individual artist or consumer of art (Parsons, 1987). These art-based considerations of child development are extensions of the educational foundations with which every aspiring teacher becomes familiar. In Piaget's "formal operational" stage (11 and older), children can think logically about abstract propositions (Inhelder & Piaget, 1958). A prime example is the fifth grader considering whether she would drink beer 8 years from now. However, not all children think and reason the same way, nor should we force them to do so. Making comics is one way for students to work through abstract circumstances one panel at a time.

The most noted advocate for a strong link between learning and life was John Dewey. For example, Dewey (1916) wrote: "A being connected with other beings cannot perform his own activities without taking the activities of others into account" (p. 14). Comics, and the process of creating such works, connect students in unique and stimulating ways. Students must consider the activities of others when they collaborate but also when they present, exhibit, and provide feedback. But Dewey was also concerned with the intellectual freedom of an individual: "A progressive society counts individual variations as precious since it finds in them the means of its own growth. Hence a democratic society must, in consistency with its ideal, allow for intellectual freedom and the play of diverse gifts and interests in its educational measures" (p. 357). The demand on educators to address the dynamics of a classroom alongside the needs of an individual can be extremely challenging, especially for inexperienced teachers. Activities such as designing comics in class are a good conduit for helping teachers to connect with their students, and for students to connect with themselves.

A final consideration of Dewey and *Democracy and Education* (1916)—he considered the practical implications of his philosophies and theories: "The problem of instruction is thus that of finding material which will engage a person in specific activities having an aim or purpose of moment or interest to him, and dealing with things not as gymnastic appliances but as conditions for the attainment of ends" (p. 155). Rather than the packaged curricula with rigid structures so common in our classrooms, Dewey advocated a more organic, personalized approach to curriculum and instruction. The current focus on test preparation—perhaps the ultimate example of "gymnastic appliances"—undermines efforts toward independent and original thinking. Teachers now have to work all the harder to engage children in the learning process. Creating comics is one source of engaging, project-based learning with tangible linkages to important academic skills and standards. An as example, an art teacher in Cleveland reported that even though her comic book unit had concluded, her students continued to meet during lunch and after school to create their comics. These students were reaching Dewey's "attainment of ends": authentic engagement in language, texts, and creative art.

TACKLING LIFE ISSUES

When Dewey was writing in the early 20th century, he could never have imagined the 21st-century lives of our students today: from social networking to cyberbullying, video games to gang violence. Schools struggle to help students cope with difficult situations as well as embrace new opportunities. In difficult economic times, for example, rates of homelessness among students increase and teachers find themselves counseling the young victims of foreclosure and eviction (Tulenko, 2009). No graduate course or textbook can prepare a teacher for that task. What teachers can do, however, is find ways for children to synthesize difficult issues in their lives. In doing so, children realize an immediate purpose for school. And teachers suddenly have a way of introducing and reinforcing core content and basic skills. Comics writing and designing has become an effective way of simultaneously addressing learning standards and children's personal challenges.

For some students, the process is cathartic. The magazine *Teaching Tolerance*, published by the Southern Poverty Law Center, interviewed a girl from Philadelphia who was creating a comic book as part of a resource room activity (DeSimone, 2006). Her cousin was in prison, and she was working to bring some sense into her life through the creation of an original comic book. Her teacher helped her work through the story with simple daily discussions. The girl became more willing to talk about her family's situation. The teacher asked the student if she wanted to base her comic book on the story of her cousin, but the student declined. Rather, she wanted to continue talking about her cousin and make a comic book about fictional characters, with a focus on tolerance and forgiveness. Through all this, the teacher found more opportunities to reinforce spelling and grammar skills. The girl first wrote her story in paragraph form. Before setting the story into comic book panels, the teacher and student reviewed the characters and plot, and they talked about the proper construction of a compound sentence and the proper usage of semicolons. The resulting comic book was a dynamic, well-written portrayal of the girl's reflections on today and hopes for the future.

In some cases, children with similar circumstances work together to design a comic book that encapsulates comparable life struggles. For example, the youths at the KARE Family Center in Tucson are all children of incarcerated parents. Their story, titled "The Kid," portrays a young boy, representative of all the authors. The comic book begins with a description of the kid, who lives with his alcoholic mother. The authors wrote: "His mom was *broke*. So she would steal stuff to feed the kid. She got caught. They put her in jail. She didn't come home. So the kid hid under the bed for a while" (see Figure 5.5). After Child Protection Services takes the kid away, a caped superhero flies to the home of the kid's grandparents to inform them that the kid needs a home. The grandparents take custody of the kid, and he gets nutritious meals and clean clothes. They take the kid to the KARE Family Center where he meets other youths who are in the same situation. They write and draw together, and they talk with each other about their problems. The authors write about this experience: "It helps him get it off his chest. It also helps him be a better person." The comic book about the kid did more than help the children of incarcerated parents to work through difficult life circumstances. The comic book made its way into the hands of Arizona policy makers, who used the story to press for increased funding for at-risk children's services.

BREAKING LANGUAGE BARRIERS

The challenges faced by children at the KARE Family Center are extraordinary, but many students, alongside their parents and teachers, struggle with literacy needs that ultimately define a child's learning experience. The debate over bilingual versus immersion programs for English language learners (ELLs) has clouded two important facts about children new to the English language: (1) they need multiple and diverse exposures to

**Figure 5.5.
Jesus Ricardo Miranda III,
Juanita Ruelas, Larissa
Rita Ruelas, Araceli
Miranda, and Josh Frost
(second–eighth grade),
KARE Family Center,
Tucson**

language-based texts and activities (Fillmore & Valdez, 1986; Snow, Burns, & Griffin, 1998), and (2) the more time they spend engaged in English texts, the more literate in English they will become (Cummins, 2003; Krashen, 2004). A number of people have advocated for comics as a source for such English language pursuits. Cary (2004) detailed the uses of comics in a multilingual classroom and included activities designed specifically for ELLs. Krashen (2004) presented research focused on the inclusion of comics as a mainstay of free voluntary reading, which is crucial to the English skills of nonnative speakers. A number of education-focused blogs target ELLs with comic strips accompanied by comprehension strategies, summaries, and lists of words and phrases to foster fluency.

While most of the comics-based approaches for ELLs are centered on reading comic books and comic strips, the Imperial County School District in California (in walking distance of the Mexican border) is fostering English writing improvement through comics via a 3-year grant from the U.S. Department of Education. Led by the district's art coordinator, Using Sequential Art (USA) in Professional Development trains classroom teachers to create comic books as a way to improve visual art and English language arts skills, with a special emphasis on bringing ELLs to higher levels of English fluency. The students—nearly 85% Hispanic and 43% ELLs—worked in English, social studies, and science classrooms to write, design, and publish content-based comic books. The practice of synthesizing social studies through original student comics has been supported by Chilcoat (1993), who aimed to keep the historical content from becoming "boring and meaningless" (p. 113). Other students created comics about science, ranging from the causes of lightning to the importance of environmental conservation. Even mathematics comics about Measurement Man and other calculating superheroes came to life through the students' pencils and markers. The approach seems to be effective: Participating students demonstrated an increase of 5 percentage points in English language arts and 7 percentage points in math on the California Standards Test—far better than students who did not participate (Imperial County Office of Education, 2009). Examples from the USA Project are posted at http://www.comicbookproject.org/cali08a.htm

Whether in the California desert or traffic-clogged Bronx, ELLs who create original comic books often use the medium as a reflection on life. Two fifth graders from the Bronx collaborated to create a comic book titled *Bronxside Story*. A riff on *West Side Story*, this comic book features egg-shaped characters with one major difference between them: half the characters wear the Puerto Rican flag and the other half the Dominican flag. The two cultures, which share the neighborhood, are not getting along. Their members argue in the park; one of the Dominicans says to a Puerto Rican: "Get out of this park. We don't like your kind here." The argument escalates to a precipitous point, as readers brace themselves for a fight. This comic book, though brightly colored and humorous, is reflective of an all-too-familiar conflict in the Bronx. The culture clash between these two particular groups has been a point of tension for many years and has occasionally led to violence among youths (Barbanel, 1994). The comic book ends in peace, however, when a superhero named Global Man flies down to help the two groups understand how similar they are in terms of their homelands, cultures, and backgrounds. The student collaborators explained to me how Global Man represents tolerance—all the characters needed was a little help in connecting themselves to their neighbors. They wished that the same could happen in their own school and neighborhood.

LESSONS FROM THE COMIC BOOK PROJECT

Through CBP, students have examined their identities individually and as part of a larger community. In Tucson, dozens of schools, libraries, community centers, and after-school programs delved into creating and publishing comics. Workshops were held in the community centers of the Pasqua Yaqui tribe. Each workshop began with a spiritual prayer invoked by tribe members; a number of the participating educators were working with youths from the Pasqua Yaqui tribe and Tohono O'odham nation. Along with building English language arts and creative skills, they aimed to reconnect the youths with indigenous languages. In discussing the theme—"I am a superhero"—the teachers shared native legends, and we discovered synergy between ancient lore and modern superhero tales.

Between their drawings of cacti and desert scenes, the students designed characters who struggled with peer pressure in school hallways, studied to get better grades, or complained about younger siblings. Even those heroes who fought villains from faraway lands mirrored the student authors in tangible ways. One hero, RockoMan, battled an evil fairy by stringing a loud guitar across his shoulder and rocking his way to victory. One can imagine the guitar chords blaring from RockoMan's amplifier, almost as loud as the Green Day songs that emanated from the girl's headphones.

One group, called the Owl & Panther, brought together children in kindergarten through high school who were refugees. Their families had fled to the United States in pursuit of sanctuary from abuse, trauma, corruption, and devastation in their home countries. The members of the Owl &

Panther used creative activities to reflect on their pasts and hopes for the future. With a cadre of adult volunteers, ranging from professional writers to social workers, Owl & Panther's participants received hands-on instruction and advisement with all their creative projects. The organization was already experienced in publishing, having produced a volume of poetry.

However, when it came time to create a comic book, the children's enthusiasm was matched by the volunteers' apprehension—nobody had ever created a comic book before. They decided to do what they had always done in the past, which was to help the young people tell a story and be creative. And creative they were: Rather than drawing their comic book, the youths gathered photographs from their homelands and used those images as the backgrounds for their story. They wrote several drafts of the story for the comic, and they tried to match their words with the photographed images. Of course, the images on their own did not tell a story, so the youths began to alter the photos with markers, glue sticks, small screwdrivers, and other tools. They drew new faces on some of the people in the pictures; they placed their main characters into the foreground of a snapshot of a refugee camp or burned village. The comic book came to life panel by panel. With each addition to the sequence, the young refugees found a way to tell their own personal stories, and the rest of us, adults, learned a bit more about the power of creative art and writing.

STUDENT COMIC BOOK SELECTION

The owl and panther featured throughout this comic book originated from a Cherokee legend. The book begins with this legend: "When the world was new, the Creator gathered all the plants and animals." This first page of the comic book also initiates the unusual approach to comic booking by the youths and their mentors. Manually altered photographs provide the backgrounds for each panel. For the foregrounds, different youths drew animals on separate sheets of paper, then cut and pasted their drawings into the actual comic book. For the frequently appearing owl and panther, however, the group used a preprinted set of the characters and changed their size and color according to the storyline. Another interesting element of the first page is the dichotomy between the narrated captions and word balloons. The captions are typed on a computer, while the animals' dialogue is handwritten. The varied approach to text development enables the legend to stand apart from the supporting dialogue.

The youth creators of the comic book reflect on the results of human "progress" on the third and fourth pages. Darker than any of the previous

Figure Set 5. The Owl & Panther (kindergarten–adult), Tucson

When the world was new, the Creator gathered all the plants and animals.

The second night found some of the plants and animals drooping.

The next night, almost all of them fell asleep.

When the seventh night ended, it was just the Owl and Panther and a few plants like the pine, the hemlock, the cedar, the spruce, the laurel and holly who were still awake.

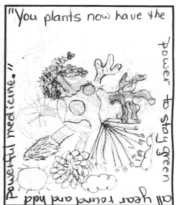

In El Salvador children didn't have a safe place to play.

There was corruption...

in MALI

Children were taken as Soldiers

in UGANDA

There was WAR

in CAMEROON

pages, here the group shows how the earth was mistreated. The powers of the owl and panther were ignored—"whole cultures and peoples were destroyed." The youths then relate the story to their home countries. The middle of the page shows a makeshift memorial as a result of the dictatorship's bloodshed. Armed militiamen on the street and in helicopters gun down innocent women in the name of "justicia." A similar scene unfolds in Guatemala: "Y asi muere nuestro pueblo." The selected photograph features soldiers trampling over the lush fields as children look on. The etched lines around the children and soldiers make them appear electrified with tension. The artists color the space over the home in blood red, parallel to the traditional *traje* that connects the last two panels of the page. The theme continues on the next page, featuring the insecurity in El Salvador, corruption in Mali, abductions in Uganda, and war in Cameroon.

The comic book concludes not in these ravaged places, but in Tucson, at the Hopi Foundation's Center for Prevention and Resolution of Violence (CPRV) and the University of Arizona's Amy Shubitz Clinic, named after a visionary community leader who aided torture victims. These support systems, along with the staff and volunteers of the Owl & Panther, have offered a second chance for children in some of the most unenviable and desperate situations. They gave the children a voice and empowered the youths to conclude the comic book with some powerful words:

> The spirit of the owl and panther inspired these children to be brave and creative. By telling their stories, the children help others to find their own healing powers . . . and their work continues. In Tucson, AZ the refugees write themselves out of their darkness.

To read the full-length, color version of this comic book, visit www.ComicBookProject.org/wcmk.htm.

CLASSROOM APPLICATION

The Owl & Panther's comic book uses photographs as backgrounds. This example can be a springboard for a memoir/community learning approach to creating a comic book in a classroom. There are numerous ways to go about such an activity—the youths in Tucson used photographs that had been collected from their families and the adults at the organization. Because students might have limited access to personal photos, the activity below uses a different approach. Students here use digital cameras to capture the scenes of the comic book.

Activity:

Going Digital with a Comic Book

Goal:

To build an artistic-written sequential narrative through the exploration of digital media.

Handout:

Digital cameras, construction paper, typing paper, black pencils, and colored pencils.

Procedure:

Students should draft a manuscript for their comic books, just as they would with a hand-drawn comic. Once the manuscripts are complete, however, instead of drawing the comics, they will stage each of the scenes (or panels) and take digital photos. Students should consider the background and foreground for each panel, just as they would a conventional comic book. Then they can take multiple photos of each scene.

Once the photos are taken, students can select which ones make the cut for the comic book, print them out, and paste them onto the construction paper. They can write their text by hand or type it on computer directly on digital photo files or on typing paper. This approach to comic book making incorporates elements of drama production, digital photography, and desktop publishing.

Thought Questions/Discussion Ideas:

1. Along with digital cameras, what are some other ways to use technology to create a comic book?
   (Flatbed scanners for artwork, software [e.g., Photoshop] to manipulate images, the Internet to upload new comics)
2. How does using a camera to create your panels impact how you think about color, space, atmosphere?
   (You have to consider everything you would in hand-drawing a comic book, but use a different tool to do so.)
3. What will your cover look like?
   (Your cover should entice the reader to open the comic book and read it. Think about how your cover will look before you start drawing it.)

Extra Activities:

1. Add some design to the borders of your comic book.
2. At the bottom of the very last page, write a sentence about why it is important to resolve conflicts peacefully.
3. On a separate sheet of paper design a public service announcement about your community that could be inserted into your comic book.

CLASSROOM RESOURCES

Internet resources related to comics and ELLs:

http://archiecomics.com/podcasts
http://eslarchie.wordpress.com
http://eslcomics.blogspot.com

Comics—memoirs, biographies, and other nonfiction texts—focused on tackling difficult life issues:

Elementary school level:

Siegel, S. C., & Siegel, M. (2006). *To dance: A ballerina's graphic novel.* New York: Simon & Schuster.
Stamaty, M. A. (2004). *Alia's mission: Saving the books of Iraq.* New York: Knopf.

Middle school level:

Delisle, G. (2005). *Pyongyang: A journey in North Korea.* Montreal: Drawn & Quarterly.
Jacobson, S., & Colon, E. (2006). *The 9/11 report: A graphic adaptation.* New York: Hill & Wang.

High school level:

Guibert, E. (2009). *The photographer.* New York: First Second.
Torres, A. (2008). *American widow.* New York: Villard.

CHAPTER 6

Publishing and Presenting

Children spend many hours over the course of several months planning, writing, and designing their comics. They agonize over the drafts, crossing out characters and erasing dialogue better suited for elsewhere in the comic. They consult with peers on the direction of the story and compromise some of their own ideas to make room for others. They delicately outline the foregrounds and backgrounds in pencil and then carefully ink those lines with black pens and markers. They use colored pencils to bring the comics to life with splashes of the color palette. In time, they design a cover to represent the comic book—a curtain to be drawn before the action begins. And with all that work, it would be a true indignity for the end result to be filed in a cabinet or, worse, the wastepaper basket.

Publishing is an important, and often overlooked, element of the writing process. For professional comics creators, there has been a recent renaissance of self-publishing with the advent of web comics and short-run print services. These two factors have also enabled small, independent comics publishers to thrive. For students, publishing their work enhances extrinsic motivation. A student publication of comic books—or any written work—validates and celebrates the effort that young people put forth. They get to see their names in print alongside their art and writing. Their parents and friends can marvel at these end products and share them for years to come. The students can touch and feel the results of the time invested in creating the comics, a rare tangible outcome of schoolwork. Yet the physical effect is usually overmatched by the emotional impact; I have seen many wide-eyed children gasp at the sight of their comics in print. One student in Connecticut, in tears and with a citywide publication in hand, said to me, "I don't want to open the cover, just to make this last."

But in another sense, publishing is an intrinsic motivator, inspiring students to write more and eventually publish more. Calkins (1994) explains: "Publication . . . is the *beginning*, not the *culmination* of the writing process. Publication does not mean that the process is over, that children can now gaze at their monuments. Instead, publication inducts us as insiders into the world of authorship" (p. 266). This is certainly the case when children produce comic books, because, as is the nature of a comic book series, the authors extend their characters over several publications. Children fully expect themselves to write another issue in the series, which is why so many of the student comic books conclude with "To Be Continued." The young authors are not lacking quality endings to their comics. Rather, they are enticing their readers to stay tuned for more. In short, publication is the end of one comic book and the springboard for another—a number of students participating in CBP for multiple years have maintained their characters from comic to comic, even though the designated themes changed. For example, a student from New York City invented a character with telepathy who could communicate with animals to help save the environment. The following year this character used his special mind to communicate with elected officials when the theme revolved around community. The year after that, the character "mind spoke" with ATM machines when the theme changed to financial literacy. Each year the character matured, as did the student's writing skills and creative development.

Along with building both extrinsic and intrinsic motivation for students, publishing student comic books is a bridge to core writing skills and mechanics—Elbow (2002) insisted: "Publication is the single strongest way to help encourage students to revise and copyedit" (p. 5). Because publishing is that part of the writing process in which an author makes a piece of writing public, students want to represent themselves in the best possible light. They do not want peers and family members to see spelling and punctuation errors in the comics. Similarly, they do not want their published comics to feature stick figures or plain backgrounds. Students are inspired to create quality work not for a grade or a test score but when they know that the work will find an audience. This is all the more important in a group project. When one member of a comic book team lacks focus or motivation, other members often chide the idler into action. I witnessed one boy say to his teammate who seemed to be slacking: "Come on, man! People are gonna see this thing!" Those words prompted a new burst of energy from the entire team.

MODELS OF PUBLICATION

When people hear the word *publication*, they often imagine a glossy, bound book produced by professional text setters and graphic designers. However, there are a variety of models for publishing student comics, and many sidestep the costs of a professionally set and printed work. As with music, many youths now get their comics over the Internet, so it is natural for them to publish their own works online. Of course, the cost of publishing online is either negligible or free, an enticing prospect for teachers. However, there is still value in a printed piece, notably highlighting the importance of books in a young person's life. Furthermore, a printed comic book is a physical testament to the students' hard work and achievements— something that can be immediately celebrated by parents, administrators, and other important stakeholders. The decision of how to publish student comics depends on the needs and resources of a particular classroom. The most important thing is that the comics get published, one way or another. The following section highlights some models of publishing with a practical focus on the everyday concerns of educators.

The Zine Model

Zine is short for *fanzine*—a self-published collection of writing and imagery born out of the punk rock movement of the 1970s and 1980s. Guzzetti and Gamboa (2004) investigated teenage girls' use of zines to advocate for social justice and denigrate mainstream popular culture. From an educator's perspective, these girls were producing written works on their own time and with their own resources, an indication of their commitment to literary communication. With some blank paper, pens, scissors, and glue—likely replaced by computers nowadays—zine makers head to the photocopy machine to print on demand for friends and a community of like-minded readers. Like comic books, zines are serialized in the sense that they feature multiple issues and address ongoing themes.

The zine publication model is easily replicated in the classroom. Students create comic strips or pages from comic books that are compiled into a weekly, biweekly, or monthly black-and-white production and photocopied at the school. There are some distinct advantages to this publishing model. First, it allows for multiple publications throughout the process of comics development. Rather than a culmination of student comics, the zine model highlights comics in progress. Students publish their comics all along the way, building excitement for the stories and a growing readership in and of the school. In essence, the zine model multiplies the motivational power of publishing. Another advantage of the zine model is that it puts students themselves in charge of the publication. By definition, a zine is self-published, and a comics zine in the classroom should be no different. A teacher can help oversee aspects of the process and facilitate access to the photocopier, but the bulk of the publication rests in the hands of the students.

Along with self-published comics in the Western world, there is precedence for zinelike comics publishing in Japan: *doujinshi* (Bitz, 2009a). Japanese fans of manga produce original comics and then photocopy those works for friends in their *doujinshi* circles. They also bring their self-published comics to large conventions devoted to amateur comics development. Even some professional manga creators introduce their new works as *doujinshi* to get initial feedback on the characters and stories—a ready-made test market for fresh concepts. Especially for young manga fans in the classroom, establishing a *doujinshi* circle in school can be motivating. Of course, the circle need not include manga exclusively. Students can decide what makes the cut, as long as the process is fair and inclusive.

The Culmination Model

The very positive aspect of the zine model—frequent publications throughout the course of comics development—also can be a detriment. When the comics are finished, there is relatively little fanfare over the completed product. The culmination model, on the other hand, compiles completed student comics in a printed piece at the close of the school year—a nice way to celebrate the students' efforts in conjunction with an exhibit or presentation. The culminating publication can be printed in black and white; however, if students design their comics in color, it is ideal to print the publication in color. The publication can include photographs of the students alongside their comics, as well as front and back matter listing people to thank (e.g., the principal and superintendent). Desktop publishing software such as Adobe InDesign or Quark is useful for designing such publications, but they can also be produced with Microsoft Word or other word processing software.

The prime disadvantage to culminating publications is the cost, although the Internet enables a teacher to collect price quotes from a variety of vendors. CBP uses an online service called Ad-Graphics (www.ad-graphics.com), which generates an instant quote from printing criteria, including page size, page count, binding type, and quantity. Still, the cost can be prohibitive for many schools. However, there are ways to raise funds for a culminating publication. Just as schools sell advertising space in their yearbooks and concert programs, the same can happen in a comic book publication. In fact, students can custom design the advertisements, fostering a connection between students and the business community and reinforcing some important career skills. A school could also sell its culminating comics publication as a fund-raiser to cover the printing costs or supplies for the comics club. Personally, I would much rather buy an original comic book from a student than a candy bar or cheese log.

Related to the printing costs, another challenge of the culmination model is including every student's comic in the publication. If every student in a class of 25 creates an eight-page comic book, the culminating publication would be 200 pages—untenable for even the most well-funded school. To reduce the page count, teachers elect to include a single page, or sometimes a single panel, from each student so that everyone can be represented. However, this approach undermines the very comics on which the students work so hard. Readers only get a taste of the characters and the writing, without fully appreciating the narratives, arguably the most important aspect of the student work. One solution is to have students work in groups, as discussed in Chapter 4, not only for the sake of collaborative learning but also for the practical consideration of producing a culminating publication. Another solution is to have a competition for the three or four spots in the publication for full-length comics, with other students published with a select page or panel. The competition could be anonymous and judged by an independent panel of teachers or students for the sake of fairness. Of course, some teachers may be uncomfortable with eliciting such rivalry among students and, therefore, look to another publication model.

Citywide/Districtwide Publications

Schools can pool their resources for a culminating publication by including comics from students across a city or district. One of the exciting aspects of this model is that it features a diverse range of work from a variety of sources. Students can read stories from other comics creators in another school or neighborhood and feel an instant connection through the art, writing, and stories. Citywide or districtwide publications become vehicles for communication between youth creators and readers, particularly if the schools involved base their comics initiatives on the same theme. Such a model can elicit some surprising results. In New York City, for example, CBP has published an annual citywide publication for 8 years, and the issues raised by students in those theme-based comics vary depending on the borough and neighborhood in which the students live. For example, when the theme was based on environmental protection, the culminating publication featured a comic book about landfills from a group of students in Staten Island near the now defunct Fresh Kills landfill. In contrast, students near the beach in Far Rockaway, Queens, created a comic book about beach erosion and water pollution.

A significant challenge with citywide and districtwide publications is coordination. If multiple schools submit their work for publication, the stack of comics can grow very quickly. Someone needs to organize the comic books, log in the entries, establish a judging panel, collect and tabulate the judges' scores and comments, notify selected students, make sure that student names are spelled correctly, collect release forms, scan the comics for printing, oversee the layout and design of the publication, find a printing vendor, and distribute the printed copies of the comic before the close of the school year. Parent and teacher volunteers can be helpful with these tasks, but a dedicated coordinator for such an effort is indispensable. CBP has regularly relied on graduate assistants, who have traveled many miles to collect comics from participating schools.

Web Publishing

Another publication model that works for many schools is usually cost free: web-based publications. Web publishing can be accomplished via a school's website or free web-hosting services offered through Google, Yahoo, and other companies. Students are also keen to publish their comics on social networking sites such as Facebook and MySpace, but many schools block such sites because of concerns about adult content. For comics to be posted on the Internet, the pages need to be scanned at a relatively low resolution—less than 100 dots per inch (dpi)—so that the files are not too large to view or download. Each page of a comic can be posted as a thumbnail, which viewers click for a larger version. Alternatively, the pages can be compiled into a PDF file, which makes it simple for readers to view and print in full. However, if the comics are going to be posted as a PDF file for the purpose of printing, they should be scanned at a higher resolution—at least 200 dpi.

The global aspect of web publishing becomes a motivator for many students. One teacher told his class: "Remember, people from all over the world will see your comics: Africa, China, South America . . ." As he listed the faraway places, the students' eyes widened before the entire class eagerly jumped into the dialogue writing activities assigned for the day. Also, due to the flexible nature of web-based publishing, many schools are able to upload revised versions of the students' comics without incurring expensive printing costs. Because of issues such as those mentioned above, several educators have advanced student publishing on the Internet as a beneficial literacy application, among them Black (2005), Chandler-Olcott (2008), Condon and McGuffee (2001), Gentry (2008), and Heyer (2009).

Teachers can take advantage of the Internet to not only publish student comics but also guide the project all along the way. A teacher in Bridgehampton, New York, for example, used the free service from Google to set up a classroom website and manage his comic book project: http://mrtomhouse.googlepages.com/thecomicbookproject. He posted assignments and due dates so that students could stay on track with the intermediate steps of the process. He included hyperlinks to resources and web pages, which the students could use to learn new techniques and generate ideas related to their comics. He also posted excerpts from the completed comics, along with a link to the school's gallery on the CBP website, which includes photographs of the students hard at work. While the students in Bridgehampton created their comics without digital technology, their teacher capitalized upon the advantages of new technologies and their assets in project management, data collection, and alternative modes of publishing.

The resources section of this chapter includes tools for web publishing, including some websites where students can create their comics online.

PRESENTING AND EXHIBITING

Publishing comics is one facet of promoting student work; presenting and exhibiting the comics is another. By establishing public displays of the comic books, educators help students celebrate their processes and achievements with peers, family members, and community members. Presentations also allow students from different schools and neighborhoods to share their comics and the ideas contained therein. In other words, these presentations become large-scale authors' circles where the students talk about what they created and comment on the work of others (Harste, Short, & Burke, 1988). This can be a formal process during which designated students meet to discuss their characters and storylines. More often, though, the formation of an authors' circle at a comic book exhibit is informal; like-minded students gather around the comics that they admire and confer about the merits of the work.

Displaying the Comics

There is no one correct method of displaying the student comics at a presentation, but at CBP we've found it is important for students and other attendees to be able to open and read the books. Even though the displayed comics are original works, they should not be behind glass or enclosed in an exhibit case. The students created the comics to be read, not to be admired from afar or behind a rope as in a museum. The many exhibits established by CBP have demonstrated the reverence and delicateness with which people approach original student-generated comic books—not one has been marred during an exhibit. That said, it is also important to display the comics in such a way that they remain fixed to a wall or table. For wall displays, we punch a small hole into the corner of each comic, tie a string through the hole, and then tack the string to the wall. For tabletop displays, we use metal typing stands with magnets that hold the back page of the comics to the stands. Both these methods enable people to read the comics in a safe, nondestructive manner.

Event Planning

CBP exhibits have taken place in schools, public libraries, community centers, bookstores, universities, art galleries, children's museums, and lobbies of local government buildings. The location has been less important than the time of the event; we learned to schedule exhibits between 5:00 and 7:00 p.m. so that parents could attend and bring younger siblings, who typically tail their older brothers and sisters around the exhibit in awe. We ask students to dress nicely (no jeans or sneakers), and we often request that students come prepared to speak about the comics that they created. Students featured at the exhibits are announced by name and receive an award as well as comic books and graphic novels donated by generous publishers. In essence, the goal has been to make as big a splash as possible about these comics and the youths who created them. These events are celebrations of writing, art, narrative, community, and the learning process in general. These are opportunities to demonstrate to the children that their time and efforts are valuable and can lead to wonderful opportunities in school and in life. Rather than relegating the completed comics to a file cabinet, educators should share them with as many people as possible.

School "Cons"

A mainstay of comics culture is conventions (or "cons") such as Comic-Con in San Diego and New York City, Comiket in Japan, and many indie regional comic book conventions. Dedicated comic book fans and creators come together at these events to discuss, share, and celebrate comics. The attendees get to know each other over time, and they learn about different issues related to local communities of comic book readers and writers.

Several schools have initiated their own comic cons. As with the large-scale festivals at convention halls, the students transform their cafeterias or gymnasiums into showcases of original, cutting-edge comics. They present their comics to attendees (usually parents), who buy the works as a fund-raiser for the school. The comics educator Alex Simmons has even launched Kids' Comic Con, which takes place annually at Bronx Community College in New York City. Admission for students under 17 years old is free, and attendees are encouraged to bring their comics to share with peers and the Portfolio Review Crew—adult professionals who provide feedback and advice to aspiring young comic book developers.

Launching a school-based comic con encourages school administrators to support a comic book initiative. They witness the finished works on display alongside the students themselves setting up booths, greeting attendees, and generating excitement from parents and neighbors about a learning initiative inside the school walls. As with a school concert or sporting event, a con promotes school pride, yet in this case with a direct relationship to literacy building. Principals often give the opening remarks to a con and one principal even created her own comic strip to put on display. Hence, rather than an initiative confined to a particular classroom, a comic con brings an entire school together through the comics medium.

Marketing the Event

Whether it is a library exhibit or schoolwide con, it is important to market the event so that people attend. It would be disappointing for students to invest so much time and energy into their comics only to stand among themselves at a presentation or exhibit. There are some simple but effective marketing outlets, such as school and town websites, the events pages of local newspapers, and community announcements on local radio stations. Printed invitations and postcards for parents and community members also help to raise awareness. CBP prints postcard announcements through an online service at http://www.overnightprints.com: 1,000 full-color postcards for just over $100. School cons and comics exhibits have also proved to be popular stories for local media to cover. For example, through a simple press release, a comic book celebration in Tucson was covered by six different media outlets, including newspapers, radio stations, and television stations. The students were interviewed by professional journalists and stood before live television cameras—certainly inspiring for the young comic book creators.

Aside from bringing attention to a comics initiative, marketing also provides some good opportunities for literacy building. Students can write a letter to local council members, a press release to a newspaper, a presentation proposal for the school principal, invitations for parents and other potential attendees, a plan for how the event will be organized, the text for a flyer to post around the school, and on a community blog to raise awareness about a scheduled event. These activities are especially useful assignments for students who finish their comics ahead of others in the class, or students who do not want to work on a comic book at all. The "marketing team" can use a variety of media and resources to accomplish their tasks and learn some valuable career and business skills along the way. Especially on the high school level, a partnership could be formed with a business or entrepreneurship class whose students use the comics as a product to be developed and marketed inside and outside the school.

LESSONS FROM THE COMIC BOOK PROJECT

Every CBP program's publication and exhibit process has a story unto itself. In Philadelphia, an exhibit was held at the small but gracious Nicetown Public Library, where the comics were fastened to poster boards attached to easels. The easels had to be placed in the aisles of library books. Hence, we opted to arrange the comics by age of the student creators and then place the easels in an aisle of books appropriate for that age. During the exhibit, it was exciting to see the students go from comic book to library book and back again. In contrast, the annual New York City celebrations at the luxurious Barnes & Noble at Lincoln Center bring students, parents, and teachers from the outer boroughs of the city into the Upper West Side of Manhattan. They ascend numerous escalators and are ushered like royalty into the event room, banked with enormous windows overlooking Alice Tully Hall and the Juilliard School. The stage where they receive their awards has been shared on other evenings by famous authors such as Frank McCourt, Elmore Leonard, and Toni Morrison.

One of the most rewarding elements of these and other comic book celebrations is the opportunity for children to speak about their work. A group of children enter the stage or come to the podium and talk about their characters and storylines. They also discuss their roles in the process—which students developed the story, which designed the art-work, which were responsible for the writing. The most effective of these presentations are well prepared ahead of time. Students write notes for themselves on index cards, and they rehearse a transition to the next student speaker. Some students use multimedia tools such as PowerPoint or a slide show to demonstrate how the comic developed from a draft to the finished product. Obviously, these kinds of presentations go well beyond the realm of comics and could pertain to any subject matter. But because the students are excited about their comics, they put some extra effort into these presentations, often including their plans for the next comic book in a series.

Another effective presentation method, especially in relation to school cons, has been panel discussions. The students sit at a long table with microphones, each student with a comic book on display at the front of the table or around the room. After the students introduce their comic books, they field questions from the audience. Some audience members have asked students to explain their motives for a storyline or to describe their influences. All of a sudden, the students are talking about themselves via their comics—ideas, values, beliefs, hopes for the future, concerns about the neighborhood. Most students are conscious of how their comics address these issues, and they are eager to make those connections for others who might not be able to discern such information from the art and writing. As discussed in Chapter 5, the comics represent aspects and identities of the students who created them; a panel discussion can be a vehicle for students to explore these identities in light of comments and questions from other students or audience members.

Crucial to the success of any CBP exhibit has been the attendance and participation of parents. Parents often arrive at the celebrations, invitation in hand, without much knowledge of what their children had accomplished in creating comics. Then seeing the comics on display and hearing the presentations related to those works, parents are regularly astounded by the achievements of their daughters and sons. These exhibits also serve as an opportunity for parents to connect with each other. After one exhibit at the end of the school year, a group of parents decided among themselves to run a summer comic book club to keep the children engaged in this pursuit. The club would meet at different homes, depending on the parents' work schedules. As with any school function, parents are great volunteers at a comic book exhibit, often arranging for local sponsorships, donations of refreshments or books, and the distribution of invitations and marketing materials.

STUDENT COMIC BOOK SELECTION

Many student comic book publications and exhibits are centered on themes, as discussed in Chapter 7. This selected comic book was one of 10 to appear in a national CBP publication on the theme "leadership." In this case, numerous high school students from the St. Louis Red Cross Friday Youth Corps—an after-school program focused on community service—inserted themselves into the comic as exemplary leaders. At the top of the second page they illustrate their faces above their names. Then at the bottom of the third page they each assign an adjective to represent a personality trait: *communicative, confident, flexible,* and so on. They use these skills as volunteers, working together as a team to maximize "the power of one." Their unique personal abilities come in handy when they need to collaborate in an effort to save the city from a major disaster.

Along with this comic book from St. Louis, teachers from around the country submitted their students' comics for the national publication. The range of stories, artistic styles, and characters was astonishing. Work from students in kindergarten through high school filled the mailroom at Teachers College, and each new package offered another surprise. The comics encompassed autobiographies of the student creators, biographies of notable figures, science fiction fantasies, lunchroom dramas, tributes to family members, monster attacks on the city, and on and on. Some schools used colored pencils and others crayons. Some used the project templates, and others designed their own panels. Some created a single comic book as a class, others in small groups, and others as individuals. In looking at all these comics in their totality, however, there were three common threads running throughout the stories, whether based on an historical figure or an alien superhero: (1) leaders are important, (2) the world needs more leaders, and (3) all people have the power to be leaders if they look inside themselves.

We used a rigorous evaluation process to select which student comics would appear in the national publication. The process began with hiring six experts who would evaluate the comics in the areas of literacy, creativity, and development of the theme (leadership). After a brief training session, the panelists practiced scoring 12 comics representing different grade levels. Their scores were submitted to a two-way analysis of variance to determine inter-scorer reliability estimates—a test to ensure that the scorers were in accordance with one another. From the results of the analysis, the composite reliability coefficients were obtained using the formula that follows (Guilford, 1965):

Figure Set 6. Vik Bijanki, Lucy Chang, Lynne Christenson, Scott Frawley, Frank Hartfield, Prachi Mayenkar, Shay Merritte, Will Perry, Amit Shintre, Michael Wilson, and Drenda Underwood (ninth–twelfth grades), Red Cross Friday Youth Corps, St. Louis

$$r = \frac{V_r - V_e}{V_r}$$

where V_r = variance among scores and V_e = variance among residuals. The overall reliability coefficient was .8613, or 86%, which was deemed sufficient. Then the panel of reviewers culled through stacks of impressive comics, scoring them according to demonstrated writing quality, artistic development, creativity, and depth. Eventually the reviewers agreed on which comic books would appear in the publication. The result was an 80-page compilation of student comics titled *We, the Leaders*, which can be downloaded for free at http://www.ComicBookProject.org/pubsnf.htm

To read the full-length, color version of this comic book, visit www.ComicBookProject.org/wcmk.htm

CLASSROOM APPLICATION

Planning a school comic con takes a lot of preparation, but it can also be a wonderful learning experience for students. This activity focuses on the marketing piece for a con. Obviously, it is important for people to come to the event, and marketing is the cornerstone for high attendance and overall success.

Activity:

Planning a School Comic Con

Goal:

To build writing, interpersonal, and business skills through the planning and marketing of a school-based comic con.

Handout:

A planning worksheet that addresses the following questions:

- What do we want to accomplish with our con?
- When will the con take place?
- Where will the con take place?
- How will the event be structured?
- How will the comics be displayed or featured at the event?
- What kinds of permissions do we need to hold the event?
- Who is our target audience?

- How will we reach this audience?
- What resources do we need for the con to be successful?
- How will we involve parents? Other students? School administrators? Community members?

Procedure:

Present the concept of holding a school comic con, and have students brainstorm some ideas related to such an event. Then distribute the planning worksheet with the questions above and other questions that may be pertinent to your particular community. Introduce the concept of marketing—that is, promoting the event and garnering as much interest and attendance as possible. Consider grouping students into different teams for the event, such as the planning committee, the marketing team, and the setup crew. Designate specific times for the teams to meet in order to accomplish important tasks and assignments.

Just as the students in St. Louis each assigned themselves a character trait that would better the entire team, have each student think of a personal trait or skill that would help make the con a success. You can list these skills next to each student's name at the front of the class. If students get stumped by a particular issue in planning the con, they can look to the list of skills to find another student in the class who could help solve the problem.

Thought Questions/Discussion Ideas:

1. What personal skills or traits make for a good marketer?
   (Speaking skills, social skills, creative problem solving, ability to work with others.)
2. What are some elements of comics that could help promote a school's "con"?
   (The cover designs could become posters. The storylines could be featured on invitations or postcards.)
3. What are some innovative activities that could take place at the con?
   (Author signings, a collaborative comic book by all attendees, panel discussions.)

Extra Activities:

1. Keep a planning log or journal for the con that tracks your progress from the first day of planning to the event itself.

2. Develop a web page for the con that features excerpts from comics, pictures, a blog, and so on.
3. Use a digital video camera to film the con, and create a brief documentary about what was accomplished.

CLASSROOM RESOURCES

Books in relation to student publishing and presenting, including technological resources:

Herrington, A., Hodgson, K., & Moran, C. (Eds.). (2009). *Teaching the new writing: Technology, change, and assessment in the 21st-century classroom.* New York: Teachers College Press.

Ohler, J. B. (2008). *Digital storytelling in the classroom: New media pathways to literacy, learning, and creativity.* Thousand Oaks, CA: Corwin Press.

Richardson, W. (2009). *Blogs, wikis, podcasts, and other powerful web tools for the classroom.* Thousand Oaks, CA: Corwin Press.

Internet resources for creating and publishing comics:

http://www.professorgarfield.org/pgf_comics_lab.html
http://www.makebeliefscomix.com
http://www.pixton.com
http://www.mashon.com/comics

Web-based comics:

Elementary school level:

http://inverloch.seraph-inn.com
http://www.earthsongsaga.com

Middle school level:

http://www.tencentticker.com/butterflycomics
http://www.thedreamlandchronicles.com

High school level:

http://directionsofdestiny.com
http://requiem.seraph-inn.com

CHAPTER 7

Classrooms, Communities, and Comics

T he publications and exhibits discussed in Chapter 6 establish a sense of community inside and outside the classroom. Building community ties through the development of comics is synergistic with the very roots of public education. Along with reading, writing, and arithmetic, the earliest American schools were devoted to the needs of the particular community in which they were situated. Hence, at the start of the 20th century, rural schools taught first graders how to "thresh buckwheat, disk potatoes, plow, harrow, and plant wheat" (Clapp, 1939, p. 132). Urban schools, on the other hand, began to establish vocational programs for students in local industries such as woodworking and steel manufacturing. These two models—urban and rural—eventually led to the community school movement (Decker, 1972). Community schools remain open well after the last school bell rings as well as on weekends; community schools work with nearby organizations to provide health services, family counseling, arts instruction, and recreation activities. Not coincidentally, a number of community schools have participated in CBP through the Children's Aid Society, one of the most committed supporters of the community school model.

Along with the work of these community schools, after-school programs have been largely responsible for connecting youths to their communities through all kinds of youth media, including comic books. The Harlem Education Activities Fund (HEAF) in New York City, for example, brings middle schoolers together after school and over the summer to reflect upon the very meaning of community. One of their activities was to create comic books about Harlem and then distribute those works through a self-published compilation called *Our World, Our Responsibility*. Figure 7.1 shows an excerpt from one of their comics. The students, who had little experience with comic book design, worked with a professional comic

Figure 7.1. Nick Duffy and Nile Graham (seventh grade), Harlem Education Activities Fund, New York City

book artist to help them transform their ideas into comics. The community issues became intertwined with fantasized stories in draft form; the instructor helped the students turn the drafts into completed comics. With the publication finished, the students continued thinking about the essence of a community in the largest sense of the term during summer trips to Africa, Brazil, and Ireland. There they worked with other youths, in part through comic booking, to explore differences and similarities in their lives and neighborhoods.

It is not uncommon for a community-based organization such as HEAF to hire a professional comic book designer as the instructor for an afterschool comic book club. Khurana (2005) observed Alex Simmons, mentioned in Chapter 6 as the founder of Kids' Comic Con, as he led a group of middle and high schoolers in New York City through the process of writing and designing comics. The program was hosted by the nonprofit Educational Alliance, and it brought together youths from a variety of different backgrounds and neighborhoods. Here then is yet another concept of community made evident through comics. Although the students attended different schools and lived in diverse areas of the city, they formed a new community of youths dedicated to the art and literature of comics. They introduced each other to their favorite styles, sometimes derived from manga and other times from American classics. Through it all, Alex honed the students' sense of design and awareness about the comics publishing business. A community of like-minded youths was forged.

GETTING THE COMMUNITY INVOLVED

Whether designed in school for the purposes of a comic con or out of school in a club setting, there are a number of issues to consider when focusing on a community-oriented comic book. Such a project focuses equally on community and creativity; therefore, students need to be mindful of both throughout the entire process. Attempting to infuse a sense of community once the characters and plot have already been mapped can result in a muddled message and storyline. Similarly, focusing exclusively on community issues without planning early on how those topics will play out in the comic book can result in a rushed and low-quality product—stick figures up in arms about the environment or corruption. A well-developed "community" comic book balances the intended moral or message with intriguing art, writing, characters, and storyline. This is trickier than it may sound—many well-intentioned comic books produced by publishers or advocacy groups are usually thin disguises that young readers quickly unmask as a ploy to their interests.

Creating Safe Spaces

In the context of a community-based comic book, teachers need to maintain open minds and open forums for discussions about community. In theory, educators strive for just this at all times, but empowering children to express their thoughts can lead to unexpected outcomes. I witnessed a class discussion at a middle school in Cleveland where the teacher asked students to suggest pressing community issues, which could become the basis of a comic book. As the students called out concerns like "poverty" and "crime," the teacher praised their answers and wrote them on the board. Then one student called out "immigration." The teacher paused for a moment and asked the student to clarify. The latter responded, "There are too many illegal immigrants in our community, and they are hurting the economy." There was an uncomfortable silence in the room as the teacher paused. With seeming reluctance, she turned and wrote "immigration" on the board and quickly moved to another student's suggestion.

A scenario like this highlights how messy student-driven learning can be. A teacher cannot control what a student says when given the opportunity, nor should she want to. Communities are composed of individuals, and it is valuable for students to be able to understand and appreciate differing views through art and writing in the classroom rather than through violence and noncommunication outside school walls. Especially in light of the difficult community issues that some young people face on a daily basis, a comic book (or song, video, dramatic play, and so on) is preferable to the street corner when it comes to expressing frustrations. The arts and literature have always been vehicles for personal expression and identity exploration related to "community" in the broadest sense of the term. Comics are no exception.

Working with Professionals and Volunteers

There are many opportunities for community members and organizations to get involved in and support a comic book initiative. Local comic book artists, or artists of any medium, can workshop with the students and provide feedback on the work created in class. Local authors can speak to the children about storytelling and character development. A representative from a publishing or marketing company can introduce concepts of desktop publishing, design, and technology applications. Neighborhood businesses can sponsor a publication of student comic books, perhaps advertising on the back cover, as they are known to do in school music programs or yearbooks. Libraries, museums, and community centers can host an exhibit of the comics—an opportunity to bring a new audience into these spaces. One school in Connecticut even exhibited their comics at the front of a busy supermarket at the center of town. Shoppers stopped on their way out to examine the comics, and children in particular enjoyed reading the stories rather than trailing their parents down the aisles. It is likely that those comics had more readership than any others exhibited around the country.

Some of the most fruitful collaborations with community members have featured adult volunteers, most without any experience with comics, sitting side by side with children and talking about the stories and characters. Because the volunteers are genuinely amazed at the work of the students, they offer a good amount of praise and ask plenty of questions. They ask students to share their processes, ideas, and plans for finishing the work. In this relationship, the student is the expert and has the opportunity to teach something new to an adult. Time after time, children have relished these interactions and have come away with renewed energy to hone their comics. In some cases, community volunteers have been moved to start their own comic book projects in different neighborhoods or with their own children. These volunteers become community leaders in their own right as they involve new citizens and organizations in the creative learning and community building processes.

A simple email or phone call is a good way to get professionals or adult volunteers into the classroom. Even if the first people contacted are unable to participate, they often willingly offer names of other people who may be able to help. Once a volunteer is on board, it is important to be clear about the expected goals and time commitment of such a partnership. A professional artist, for example, might want to demonstrate a painting technique or a writer may intend to introduce a new book, neither of which may be conducive to advancing a comics initiative. Discussing a specific plan with a professional or volunteer usually results in a more effective use of time. It is also important to prepare students for the role of volunteer adults. Clarifying what a volunteer will do before that person enters the classroom helps students understand how they should interact and communicate with the new visitor. Explaining the partnership to school administrators, and getting the proper clearances, is also highly advisable.

THINKING ABOUT COMMUNITY

Brainstorming ideas is crucial to any creative project; once those ideas are recorded, the comics medium requires some critical thought as to how the ideas about a community transform into sequential artistic-written narratives. A teacher can look to some well-researched techniques. Students can create a chart for *What I KNOW – What I WANT to Know – What I LEARNED*, or *KWL* (Ogle, 1989). In the context of a comic book about the community, this translates into the following: what students know about their community, what they want to know, and what they have learned after group discussions or readings. In essence, a KWL chart becomes an intermediary step for developing the ideas for a comic book. Students can also journal their ideas, taking the brainstorming to a higher level of fluency and communication alongside personal reflections that students may have not shared with a larger group (Calkins, 2003; Routman, 2000). Contrasting the introspective journaling experience, students can role-play by improvising a dramatic storyline based on items from the brainstorming list (Muschla, 1993). As the role-plays unfold, students start to renovate basic ideas into detailed storylines that become the basis for a comic book.

There are some other brainstorming ideas observed from successful comic book classrooms and clubs. One is to provide students with a "story starter"—a snippet of a storyline that encourages students to think through the arc of the story. In Baltimore, students identified graffiti as a community issue that deserved to be addressed in their comic. The teacher presented the following story starter: "James is walking down the street and sees that the side of the school has been tagged with graffiti. What did James do?" Students began calling out ideas, ranging from "James went and told the principal" to "James had a magic eraser arm that cleaned the wall." The teacher simply nodded toward the blank paper and pencils, and the students jumped into writing their stories and drafting their panels. The teacher's simple prompt jump-started the process—another reason for the term *story starter*. It is important to note some subtleties about the story starter that the teacher put forth. First, she gave the character a name (James) rather than saying, "You are walking down the street . . ." Doing so allows students to imagine a story rather than their own personal reactions to graffiti on a wall. James could be a responsible citizen, evil villain, boy with a magic eraser arm, teacher, or anything else that a student can imagine. Second, the teacher asked, "What did James do?" She did not provide multiple-choice options; she empowered the students to develop their own ideas and personal reflections on the community issue of graffiti.

WORKING WITH THEMES

When CBP first launched, students were not required to base their comics on a certain theme. Rather, we encouraged self-expression and identity exploration by asking students to create comics about what was important to them or something they would want the reader to know or understand. As I reported in *Art Education* (Bitz, 2004b):

> The authors were usually the main characters, but they rarely acted as heroes. They were often at the mercy of uncontrollable circumstances, such as a random gun shot or a hit-and-run accident. At the end of the stories, the authors remained alive, but many of their friends and relatives (real or fictionalized) had either died or been put into jail for life sentences. Some of the comic books had a moral, such as "don't do drugs," but just as many were tales of futility in which the main characters were doomed despite bold efforts to overcome struggles. (p. 34).

While this open-ended approach may be conducive to expression and akin to art therapy, it left some students wondering where to begin. The framework was too large for many students, and their stories drifted between characters and themes. From then on, CBP established an annual theme, ranging from teamwork to financial education. Even though the themes were universal, the content of the comics were typically local. For example, in a comic book about the environment, the superhero named Super Garoy saves the neighborhood of Elmhurst in Queens, New York, not the entire world (see Figure 7.2).

Given the national and citywide themes, many individual schools and after-school programs developed their own themes in order for students to connect with a community. Instructors at an after-school program run by the Caribbean American Merchants Block Association in Brooklyn asked comic book club members to focus only on the one block of their school—the theme was "the block." Students walked outside and began to see, not just look at, the storefronts. They carried notebooks and jotted down their observations. One student designed a formal survey to check off the categories of shops. With the observations collected and the survey results tallied, the students concluded that the block had plenty of liquor stores, hair-braiding salons, and bodegas, but no supermarkets, bookstores, or clothing shops. The instructors asked students what they would change about the block if they could, and the comics were on their way to development.

Some other good themes for a comic book about the community are:

- Reducing pollution
- Restoring parks or buildings
- Helping the poor or homeless
- Aiding the elderly
- Preventing crime
- Ending gang violence
- Combating animal abuse

Figure 7.2. Fernando Acevado (fifth grade), PS 89Q, New York City

LESSONS FROM THE COMIC BOOK PROJECT

Another model for volunteerism fostered by CBP has revolved around college students. Many colleges have service requirements, and comics have become a way for college students to leverage a particular skill or interest in order to help local youths. In one example of this, AmeriCorps students from Middlesex County College in New Jersey adopted CBP as a way to help young people in nearby communities create and publish comic books. The college students visited a variety of sites, ranging from low-income housing authorities to vocational high schools, and mentored school-age youths on the writing and design of comic books. The biggest challenge of this model surfaced in the college students' inexperience working with youths. They were uncomfortable at first, unsure of how to approach the children. They quickly overcame this with a common piece of advice: "Just be yourself." The relative young age of the college students quickly changed from a detriment to an asset. The college students talked freely with the youths often about popular movies, video games, and other aspects of youth culture. A strong bond was formed, and the comic books developed rapidly.

The success of this model was based largely on the college students' ability to relate to the youths and vice versa. The college volunteers regularly discussed current issues and events with the students. Because the volunteers were neither teachers nor parents and did not have an authority role, the students felt free to discuss their ideas and concerns related to comic book stories, but also to life itself. The college students became adept at helping the youths transform those life concerns into storylines, establishing a tangible link between learning and life. Without studying the theories behind community education, the college students forged a link between learning and life by encouraging individualism alongside community activism. They also become more closely tied to a community, many considering "community" for the first times in their lives.

Teachers who aim to bring college-age volunteers into the classroom can start by contacting a local college or university, perhaps with the education, English, or art departments. Many colleges also have a community relations liaison, who can be a good conduit for raising awareness on campus of volunteer opportunities. A college's student government association can also be a fruitful resource. As with adult volunteers, however, it is important to have a firm understanding with college students about what is expected of them. What skills do they bring to the classroom? Would they be more comfortable working with students one on one, in groups, or as a whole class? The answers to these questions will vary among college-age volunteers; in-person interviews well before scheduled volunteer sessions help a teacher maximize the abilities of a given college student.

STUDENT COMIC BOOK SELECTION

The two girls from New Jersey who created the bilingual comic book titled *Take Leadership If Someone Needs Your Help*!!! (*Toma Lideraje Si Alguien Necesita Tu Ayuda*) did so with the aid of college student volunteers. The context was a Spanish class, but it was no easy grade for the native Spanish speakers. Through the development of comic books, the teacher required students to simultaneously hone their writing skills in Spanish and English, as well as think critically about something that they wanted to say about "community." The students learned new vocabulary, including *una comunidad* and *el barrio*. All the while, the college students facilitated the development of the comics by working with these two particular girls on everything from writing mechanics to color selections.

The resulting comic book addresses domestic violence. Yet unlike the student comic book from Chicago that features a victim fighting against her aggressor, this comic book is told from the point of view of an outside observer—a friend who witnesses the abuse. One of the most distinguishing characteristics of the comic is the girls' use of perspective. The two girls from New Jersey did not have a lot of experience in making art, but they devised a simple yet effective technique for differentiating between foregrounds and backgrounds. They placed the images for the foreground at the bottoms of the panels and the images for the backgrounds at the tops of the panels. Doing so infused a sense of perspective and dynamicism into the comic book. They also make creative use of the thumbnail technique, also featured in the student comic book from Chapter 1. For instance, in the third panel on the first page, the creators show the back of a female character but feature the front of her face in a thumbnail. They use this technique again on the third page of the comic, homing in on the character's facial expression in the thumbnail close-up.

To read the full-length, color version of this comic book, visit www. ComicBookProject.org/wcmk.htm

Figure Set 7. Alma Rosa Villa and Miriam Rodriguez (ninth grade), Woodbridge Vocational-Technical High School, Woodbridge, New Jersey

CLASSROOM APPLICATION

One way to connect a comics project to the community is through an oral history: a collection of people's testimony about their own experiences. Children conduct interviews with family members or people in the community, and then synthesize those narratives into comics. Typically, oral histories are based on a central question or issue, such as immigrating to a new country, living in the digital age, or dealing with the impacts of climate change. Therefore, an oral history comics project is conducive to learning in the content areas such as social studies and science. This activity focuses specifically on learning more about community issues.

Activity:

Oral History Through Comics

Goal:

To use the comics medium as a platform for oral history and community awareness.

Handout:

Writing pads and pencils (or digital recorders); materials for creating comics (paper, pencils, inking pens, colored pencils)

Procedure:

Part I:

Students research some pertinent community issues through either a local newspaper or websites and then devise a central question. What is something they want to know more about in the community? Now it is time to plan the oral history project: Whom will they interview? How long will the interviews last? How will they record the data? How will they organize the data? How will they analyze the data? Next, students write the interview questions. Then they conduct the interviews. It is good practice to conduct mock interviews with other students beforehand, so that students feel comfortable with the interviewing process. (See Ritchie [2003] for more information on implementing effective oral history projects.)

Part II:

Using the interview data, students create comics about the community issue in question. The comics can directly portray the interviewees with direct quotes from the interviews; alternatively, students can depict the events or circumstances about which the interviewees speak. (Art Spiegelman's *Maus* is a good example of a comic based on an oral history, in this case from his father during the Holocaust.) The comic that the students create should reflect and synthesize the central question or issue that originally launched the project. Students can be creative in how they represent that question, whether they directly address the issue through a nonfiction account or weave the issue into a fictional narrative. In either approach, the students make use of panel structure, captions, word balloons, and all the other comics elements to demonstrate what they learned.

Thought Questions/Discussion Ideas:

1. In what ways might your own experiences affect your oral history project and resulting comic book?
    (Your own experiences and biases might affect how you interpret the interviews, but it is important to keep an open mind throughout the entire project.)
2. How will you use the interview data to formulate the comic book?
    (Writing a manuscript or outline draft will help you take the data and turn it into a story.)
3. How will the data that you collect affect the tone and atmosphere of your comic book?
    (The designs and colors should reflect the attitude of the interviewees—a somber story should be reflected in the writing style and color choices, for example.)

Extra Activities:

1. Collect and scan some photographs from each of the interviewees and work them into your comic book.
    (Be sure to return the photographs.)
2. Scan your comic book and post it to a blog related to the question or issue that you explored.
3. Present a copy of your completed comic book to each of the interviewees with a personal letter of gratitude for their time.

CLASSROOM RESOURCES

Books related to community-based education and community in the classroom:

Greeley, K. (2000). *Why fly that way? Linking community and academic achievement*. New York: Teachers College Press.

Murrell, P. C. (2001). *The community teacher: A new framework for effective urban teaching*. New York: Teachers College Press.

Umphrey, M. L. (2007). *The power of community-centered education: Teaching as a craft of place*. Blue Ridge Summit, PA: Rowman & Littlefield.

Internet resources related to community in the classroom:

http://www.childrensaidsociety.org/communityschools
http://www.ncea.com
http://www.tolerance.org

Comics that focus on the concept of community and community-related issues:

Elementary school level:

Cammuso, F. (2008). *Knights of the lunch table: The dodgeball chronicles*. New York: Scholastic.

Martin, A. M. (2006). *The Baby-Sitters Club: Kristy's great idea*. New York: Scholastic.

Middle school level:

Poe, M., & Lindner, E. (2008). *Little Rock Nine*. New York: Aladdin.

Stauffacher, S. (2007). *Wireman*. Grand Rapids, MI: Wireman Comics.

High school level:

Carey, M., & Liew, S. (2007). *Re-gifters*. New York: Minx.

Jackson, J. (2003). *Comanche moon*. New York: Reed Press.

CHAPTER 8

Launching a
Comic Book Club

There are many ways to go about creating comics in an educational setting. There is no "correct" method, as with any educational activity or curriculum. The best method is the one that meets the needs of individual students. Differentiated instruction—regarded as crucial for the ultimate success of a classroom of students—is readily obtainable in the process of making comics, simply because different students create different comics. A teacher can adapt the content of and approach to the comics based on a balance between the skills that students need to learn and those that they already possess. Because those skill sets vary between individuals, so does the approach, at least in a highly effective classroom. One student might punctuate all the captions in a comic, with a special emphasis on ending punctuation. Another student might write the dialogue for a certain villain, being sure to capture the right tone for an evil personality. Yet another student might draft a paragraph and time line in order to explain the group's plan for completing the comic book on schedule.

With all that said, there are two distinct implementation models that have emerged, resulting from two distinct learning environments: in school and out of school. In-school comic book initiatives generally transpire within the context of scheduled periods of previously existing classes. An after-school comic book club is usually an elective—one of several club options. The previous chapters have eluded to some of the differences inherent in how comics are created in school versus out of school. These divergent models are worth exploring further because both encompass a number of ideas and strategies that could benefit all students and educators.

IN-SCHOOL MODELS

An in-school comic book initiative, like the one in Cleveland described in Chapter 2, generally requires extensive support from not only teachers and students but also administrators, parents, and community members. Administrators must understand the goals and expected outcomes of the initiative. Parents need to know why their children are spending precious classroom time on making comic books. For the comic book initiative to have the most meaningful impact possible, community members should become involved in the exhibiting and promotion of the finished works.

Building Support Across Disciplines

The burden of gaining such support usually rests on the shoulders of an already stressed teacher, a common reason why a comic book project— or any creative project—gets abandoned for a more prescribed curricular package. With the permissions for an in-class comic book in place, teachers should look for ways to collaborate with each other. A multidisciplinary approach enables students to decompartmentalize learning so that the concepts cross content areas and classroom doorjambs. Students become better able to connect learning goals, assignments, and content when teachers work together to facilitate a cross-curricular project. Moreover, a multi-dimensional initiative lessens the burden on any one teacher. Say, for example, that teachers decide that students will develop comic books about space aliens who visit Earth and meet important historical figures. The brainstorming can happen in English class, the research on outer space in science class, and the development of historical characters in social studies class. (The resources section of this chapter includes some professionally published comics related to specific content areas.) While the planning of a collaboration of this nature might take some additional time and energy, the impact of the initiative is destined to be greater.

The most logical interdisciplinary connection for a comics initiative is with the art teacher. However, it is important not to assume the willing partnership of an art teacher without first discussing the project with that educator. As with any other discipline, art educators follow a set of standards and a curriculum, and they often plan their projects far in advance in order to secure necessary supplies. I have met a few English teachers who have been shocked at an art teacher's reluctance to help students create comics in art class. But consider it from the other direction— would an English teacher be happy had the art teacher popped in with a stack of comics in need of grammar and spelling revisions? If they are going to work together, English and art educators need to collectively understand and agree to the commitment necessary for a successful comics initiative.

Doing More with Fewer Resources

Scheduling the comic book process depends on what else happens in the school—everything from testing schedules to pep rallies. Teachers can elect to have an intensive approach in which the students spend every day for 3 to 4 weeks writing and designing their comics. The positive aspect of this schedule is that it immerses students in the elements of comic book literature and design. The downside is that the schedule does not allow for reflection between comic book sessions. The alternative—working on the comics once a week, for example—allows for student reflection, although students will not see finished comics until the end of the school year.

With school budgets under siege, teachers are increasingly under pressure to do more with less. Fortunately, making comics does not require expensive supplies; blank paper, lead pencils, thin black inking markers, and colored pencils go a long way. Kneaded rubber erasers work well for removing pencil lines after inking. If students are designing their own panels, rulers or other straightedges are helpful.

Technology to Create Comics

If computer technology is available, there are many ways to incorporate hardware and software into the comics process. On the simplest level, students can write their dialogue in a word processing program. They print out the pages, cut out the text for each panel with scissors, and then use glue sticks to paste the captions and word balloons onto each hand-drawn panel, as in the Owl & Panther comic book from Chapter 5. I call this "old school" cutting and pasting. This simple use of technology can be helpful for younger students or those with motor skill challenges who might get frustrated by trying to fit their writing into the confined space of a word balloon or caption box. Programs such as Microsoft Word include malleable word balloons in the "autoshapes" function.

Some teachers use Adobe Photoshop or other professional design software to help students create their comics. A few have students use electronic graphic pads and stylus pens to draw the artwork, but far more have students draw the comics with paper and pencil, then scan the artwork and manipulate the images with software. The text is easily written in Photoshop, and students can experiment with different fonts, type sizes, and effects. Figure 8.1 shows an example from a group of elementary students in New York City who used Photoshop to write and design their collaborative comic book.

Figure 8.1. Geomaris Martinez, Derek Crothers, Shanelis De La Cruz, Elhadji Thiam, Jarlene Gonzalez, Michelle Guzman, Chelsea Flete, Michelle Tineo, and Marlene Aquino (third–sixth grade), PS 161/Harlem Dowling, New York City

A number of software packages specifically designed for comics creation are available on the market. The most popular and readily affordable is Comic Life by Plasq. Students upload digital photos into the software, select panels for the layout, and then choose and manipulate word balloons and fonts as they write the text. Figure 8.2 is from an elementary school student who used Comic Life to create a comic. The student photographed Lego figures in a series of planned scenes, then added panel layouts and text with the various software functions.

Figure 8.2. Oliver Sanders (third grade), PS 372, New York City

OUT-OF-SCHOOL MODELS

When a teacher decides that his or her class will create comics, it is essentially a given that all the students will participate. There are different roles within the process, but—with rare exceptions—every student is in some way involved in the project. In contrast, an after-school program could rarely dictate such a project. As described in Chapter 1, the paradox inherent in after-school programs is that children are required to learn, but they are not required to be there. To engage students consistently, after-school programs need to offer a menu of options—clubs that children choose to attend based on their personal interests.

The children who sign up for an after-school comic book club are generally excited about comics, making art, or writing stories. However, after-school program directors and staff members can involve children who may not know where they fit into an art-making and writing process. A simple recruiting flyer that focuses a comics club on creativity and storytelling can help educators in out-of-school settings develop a youth's undiscovered skills and interests. Some of the most dedicated comic book makers are children who never demonstrated an interest in Spider-Man, Naruto, or any other comic book character. They have a story to tell, however, and that story finds an outlet in the form of a sequential artistic-written narrative.

Scheduling and Staffing the Club

Most after-school comic book clubs meet once or twice a week for about an hour. This limited time for brainstorming, writing, designing, revising, and publishing means two things. First, a successful club must be extremely organized. Youths should enter the room knowing what they need to accomplish and where the resources are to get those things done. A weekly to-do list, developed in conjunction with the club members themselves, can help students focus on these tasks. Second, a good amount of thought needs to go into the comics between club meetings. The members of an after-school comic book club can often be seen working on their comics in school, at home, on the bus—wherever they get the opportunity to further their stories and designs. The club meetings, therefore, become more like business meetings, where the young people share what they have accomplished during the week and discuss what they need to do in order to move forward with the comics before the next session. In after-school settings, the youths themselves take on much of the responsibility of developing and completing the comic book on time. In almost every case, however, there is a maniacal rush in the weeks before a publication deadline, just as in a professional publishing house.

After-school school club instructors are often college students or recent high school graduates. Although the obvious negative is that these staff do not have a lot of experience working with children, the positive is that they easily connect with the youths because the instructors are not "teaching" the club, as demonstrated in Chapter 7. They act more as mentors. They help initiate the club by putting up flyers, recruiting students, and securing the appropriate materials. They facilitate the club sessions by talking with the participants about their progress and helping them work through any stumbling blocks such as character design or sentence structure. While they may not have the skills to address all those stumbling blocks, they find the people who can help—either other participants in the club, another group leader, or perhaps a community member. After-school instructors are also instrumental in establishing exhibits and other celebrations for the comics by securing a space and helping the students prepare posters and other marketing materials.

Student-Driven Learning

The fluid nature of after-school instruction sometimes mandates an entirely different approach to teaching and learning. In a number of after-school comic book clubs, the students themselves drive nearly everything that happens during the course of the project. They form their own groups, plan the nature or theme of their comics, and delve into the process with little instructional oversight. Only motivated students with a high degree of self-direction can thrive in this environment, but most children seem able to adapt to this educational paradigm if the rules for participation are clear. Various instructors from the after-school program float in and out of the clubroom simply to make sure that the youths have everything they need to be successful. Occasionally, the adults will perform "instructional rounds" by meeting with various groups or individuals in the club for a progress report on their work and a prescription for moving forward. This is a shared responsibility among adults in the organization—a similar teaching method has been touted for school teachers by City, Elmore, Fiarman, and Teitel (2009) as a highly effective pedagogical approach.

One of the most exciting aspects of after-school comic book club is their ability to bring together youths from different parts of a community to celebrate their comics. Because most after-school programs are run by community-based organizations, community development is an important

aspect of their mission. As a result, youth participants in after-school programs are required to go beyond their schools and interact with the community. The comic book celebrations serve the function of connecting youths
from different schools in various parts of a town or city. Bonded by art and
literature, the children have an instant forum for communication—they all
participated in a parallel process leading to a dynamic display of comics.
When youths with very different backgrounds share a common experience
such as this, many of the preconceived barriers between such children seem
to fall by the wayside.

Facing Challenges

While after-school comic book clubs can lead to impressive academic
and social advancements, many face a host of challenges. First, because the
clubs are voluntary, those that do not get off to a solid start face student
attrition right away. With all the other interesting clubs available to them,
youths will not stick around for a disorganized or directionless comic book
club. Good instructors get the students excited about making comics right
at the start of the very first club session, and they maintain that energy
throughout. Youths want to know that their efforts after school will have
a tangible outcome, especially if those efforts involve extensive reading
and writing as in the comic book club. In the *Journal of Adolescent & Adult
Literacy* (Bitz, 2004a), I reported the reflections of one after-school director
about a student in her comic book club:

> He really wanted to do it, but he just got scared when he saw how much
> writing he was going to have to do. He kind of freaked out. He's been
> told he's a bad writer for so long that he just doesn't want to try anymore.
> Somebody suggested to me that I should try to get him to make a comic
> book with just pictures, and then we could add the words later or as a class
> or something. But it was too late. He didn't want to come back. (p. 579)

Another difficult challenge for after-school programs is high staff turn-
over. Most club instructors work part time for relatively low hourly wages,
and better economic opportunities often pull quality instructors away from
their sites, however reluctantly. When a club instructor leaves midstream,
many clubs fold there and then because new instructors are not privy to
the sequence established to that point. For this reason, after-school directors should require multiple staff members to be trained and knowledge-
able about the comics initiative so that another instructor can step in, in an
emergency situation.

Summer learning, an often overlooked component of out-of-school education, requires a different approach from that of the typical after-school setting. In summer programs, students generally convene every day for the entire day. This allows for an in-depth comic book experience with an intensive, uninterrupted approach to creating the comic books. For students who relish this opportunity, the experience can be transformative. In a matter of weeks, their comics come to life, as does the students' excitement about what they can accomplish as writers and artist. However, for those students who are less engaged in creating comics, the duration and intensity of a summer comic book project can be overwhelming. Summer learners should not be forced into long hours of comic book making. Other learning options should be available to them, ideally activities that the students themselves initiate as a pathway to improved learning over the summer.

ASSESSMENT

Whether in school or after school, assessment is a concern for any educator working with students on a comic book project. With so many skills represented by different roles in the creative process, assigning a grade is understandably difficult. An assessment rubric presented to students at the beginning of the process helps students to know what is expected of them. Figure 8.3 shows an example of a rubric with a five-point scale related to the following categories: character development, settings and backgrounds, plot design, writing mechanics, overall performance, and group participation. Teachers can use this rubric as a springboard for their own evaluations, depending on whether students are working collaboratively or if the comic book is centered on a specific content area.

As with most rubric criteria, the scores that a teacher assigns based on Figure 8.3 or any other rubric are subjective. Therefore, it is crucial to provide students with plenty of examples of what constitutes well-matched action and dialogue, for example. (See http://www.ComicBookProject. org/featuresnf.htm for examples of high-quality student comics.) The rubric can be a source for class discussion about the elements of a high-quality comic book versus one that needs improvement. The rubric should also help guide students as they work through the drafting and revising process. With each draft, the teacher can use the rubric as an intermediary between what the student has produced and the expected quality of work. In essence, the rubric should not be a surprise to students in a comic book

	5	4	3	2	1
Character Development	The characters are developed and designed very well; their actions and dialogue match very well.	The characters are usually well developed and designed; their actions and dialogue match fairly well.	The characters are inconsistently developed and designed; their actions and dialogue occasionally match.	The characters are rarely developed and designed; their actions and dialogue rarely match.	The characters are not developed and designed; their actions and dialogue rarely match.
Settings & Backgrounds	The setting is very clearly explained or illustrated throughout and clearly relates to the plot. Backgrounds substantially enhance the impact of the comic.	The setting is usually explained or illustrated throughout and often relates to the plot. Backgrounds generally enhance the impact of the comic.	The setting is sometimes explained or illustrated and occasionally relates to the plot. Backgrounds sometimes enhance the impact of the comic.	The setting is rarely explained or illustrated and rarely relates to the plot. Backgrounds rarely enhance the impact of the comic.	The setting is not explained or illustrated and does not relate to the plot. Backgrounds do not enhance the impact of the comic.
Plot Design	The beginning, middle, and end of the story are excellently structured with many details.	The beginning, middle, and end of the story are adequately structured with sufficient details.	The beginning, middle, and end of the story need some structural improvement and include some details.	The beginning, middle, and end of the story need some structural improvement and do not include enough details.	The beginning, middle, and end of the story need major structural improvement and do not include enough details.
Writing Mechanics	There are no mistakes in writing mechanics.	There are 1-3 mistakes in writing mechanics.	There are 4-6 mistakes in writing mechanics.	There are 5-8 mistakes in writing mechanics.	There are more than 8 mistakes in writing mechanics.
Overall Performance	The entire comic book is well-designed and well-written, and it is masterfully detailed and illustrated.	The entire comic book is mostly well-designed and mostly well-written, and it is competently detailed and illustrated.	Parts of the comic book are well-designed and well-written, but some are not. It is satisfactorily detailed and illustrated.	The comic book is only partially finished. Many panels lack sufficient detail and illustration.	The comic book is incomplete.
Group Participation	Student was an active, positive, and helpful member of the group every class.	Student was an active, positive, and helpful member of the group most of the time.	Student was an active, positive, and helpful member of the group some of the time.	Student had some difficulty working in the group, and made an insufficient contribution.	Student had difficulty working in the group, and made little or no contribution.

Total Score: _____

Comments:

Figure 8.3. Sample Assessment Rubric

project, or any other project. If a rubric assessment is to be used, it should be integrated into the process from the very beginning.

Three other kinds of assessment can be useful in evaluating student performance during a comic book project. A *self-evaluation* encourages students to write about what they learned and the effectiveness of their participation—students are typically more honest about their work than one might think. Self-evaluation tends to foster an "upward cycle" of learning (Rolheiser, 1996); self-evaluations move students to set higher goals for themselves and commit more effort to the task at hand. Regarding a comic book self-evaluation, students set goals and criteria for themselves at the outset, perhaps related to what they want their comic books to represent or what the characters will learn or experience. Then they monitor their own work, frequently checking to see if they are meeting their personal goals and criteria. A *performance evaluation* usually consists of a presentation, or perhaps a reenactment, of a comic book. Students can use multimedia tools to supplement an oral account of what they accomplished, or they can transform their comics into a dramatic play or short film. Both self-evaluations and performance evaluations can be accompanied by rubrics.

Finally, a *portfolio evaluation* can be useful for teachers and students to track the development of a comic book over the course of a semester or year. The finished comic book represents an end product, but there are many things that a student creates along the way: character sketches, plot outlines, manuscripts, penciled drafts, and more. Collecting all these assets in a portfolio demonstrates the progress (or lack of progress) that a student has made. Teachers can systematize the portfolio requirements by having students include set elements, such as at least three character profiles, a manuscript approved by the teacher, two penciled drafts, and the final comic book with full color and completed cover. This collection of "data" helps to keep the student on track and finish a comic book before a designated deadline. If students create comics in subsequent years, they can continually add to their portfolios and monitor long-term progress.

LESSONS FROM THE COMIC BOOK PROJECT

Over 52,000 students have participated in CBP nationwide. Students and their teachers or after-school instructors took the project in diverse directions, from tools for community organizing to unusual opportunities for expression by autistic youths. Rather than a step-by-step process, the project became akin to clay—easily pliable and put to many uses, shapes, and forms. Even within a given classroom, students were creating comics in diverse ways, some using computers and others pencils, some working together and others hunched over their own comics, steeped in concentration. Educators have consistently reported that although the process is time consuming, students across grade levels, skill levels, and socioeconomic backgrounds have been extremely engaged, many for the first time, in reading, writing, and making art.

While many of the project implementations have been small scale with an individual school, after-school program, or library, large-scale implementations like the ones described in this book have continued to thrive. Recently, CBP even traveled to the island of Hawaii. The first year of the Hawaii project involved a mixture of schools and after-school programs for students ranging from Grades 1 to 12. Once again, the project took on a very local flavor—students from Hawaii created comics about things that are familiar to their island: volcanic eruptions, water pollution from cruise ships, ceremonies with roots in ancient Hawaiian culture. Heroes and villains conducted their business among palm trees and black sand beaches. And yet many of the comics addressed universal issues parallel to the concerns of youths in New York, Cleveland, or anywhere else: Violence, intolerance, and poverty were common themes. The project became an opportunity for the youths in Hawaii to put their global concerns into a local perspective; the resulting comics helped them to explore their identities as Hawaiians and Americans. The students shared their comics through an islandwide publication, local celebrations, and online galleries. Their work was featured by local news media and celebrated by the superintendent's office, all of which inspired the students and their teachers to continue on with the project in subsequent years.

In the following year, the schools and after-school programs in Hawaii produced six different publications and held an array of celebrations and exhibits for students, parents, and teachers. The project has continued on in Hawaii since then, allowing students to grow with the process. Every year their comics improved, as did their writing skills and storylines. The teachers grew alongside their students; they embraced comics as a new tool to help engage their youths in literacy skill building without the tedium of worksheets or the expense of prepackaged curricula. Together, students and teachers discovered for themselves the connection between creative skills and literacy skills, and the evidence seems to show that they will continue to build those connections inside and outside the classroom for many years to come.

STUDENT COMIC BOOK SELECTION

The comic book *Friend or Foe* is a manga, or Japanese style-comic book, created by a high school student in Hawaii. There are a couple of clues, beyond the stylized hair, typical of manga design. The characters' names are Isamimaru, Riniko, and Ikinakamaru—each introduced via a panel indicating the character's name, age, and personality traits. Also typical of manga is the insertion of semiotic elements outside the images, word balloons, and caption boxes. The first page of the comic, for example, includes some Japanese writing near Isami's shoes. The introduction of Riniko, angry at Isami's tardiness, features red flames in the background. But the most fundamental aspect that makes this comic a manga is the whimsy and humor that abounds. The subject matter—bullying—is serious, but the approach is lighthearted in terms of design and narrative.

Given the nature of this comic book selection, one might assume that this comic was the result of a manga club in which every participant creates comics in a Japanese style. However, that was not the case. The comics that these high schoolers produced varied in design and direction. Rather than having a predetermined take on what a comic book should be, the students explored a range of comics and developed personal styles according to their interests and experiences. Moreover, the process of creating comics differed among students in the club. In this selection, for example, the student drew the comic by hand, inked with a black marker, and scanned the pages into a computer. She then added color with the "magic wand" and "fill bucket" tools in Adobe Photoshop. Other students, however, colored their comics with colored pencils, crayons, or markers, or chose not to color their comics at all.

The diversity of processes and results from this Hawaiian comic book club—and many others around the country—speaks to the ways in which comics can become a vehicle for personally relevant, student-driven learning. Using this comic as an example, the creator leveraged her passion for manga to engage in literacy development, artistic exploration, technological applications, and social reflections. She engaged with a community of learners within her club as well as a community of readers who experienced her work in a publication and exhibit. From the very beginning of the process to the culminating celebrations, the student was an active participant in the learning goals, curricula, and even pedagogy. She was excited to come to school and thoroughly engaged in learning. If comics can facilitate all this, there is something positive to be said for their educational viability.

**Figure Set 8. Napuaonalani Keopuhiwa (twelfth grade),
Kealakehe High School, Hawaii**

Name: Riniko
Age: 16
Female, Isami's best friend, good student, dark personlity, and speaks her mind.

To read the full-length, color version of this comic book, visit www. ComicBookProject.org/wcmk.htm

CLASSROOM APPLICATION

One of the most gratifying aspects of creating a comic book is designing the cover. The cover serves to prepare the reader for the content of the comic book, just as with a conventional book. However, for a comic book creator, the cover enables a synthesis of the characters and storyline. In *Friend or Foe*, for example, the three teenagers appear on the cover with their unique characteristics: Ikina with his headphones, Isami with the raindrop that follows him, and Riniko with her glasses and representative peace sign. Furthermore, the design of the title influences how the comic will be interpreted. The question mark and exclamation point after *friend* and *foe* puts these roles of the characters into question.

Some students, particularly the artistically inclined, desire to design the cover before planning or writing the comic book. This is generally not a good idea—a student will have a better concept of how the cover should appear after the body of the comic is complete. Additionally, the opportunity to design the cover is good motivation for completing the comic book itself.

Activity:

Designing a Comic Book Cover

Goal:

To help students synthesize their characters and storylines through the development of a comic book cover.

Handout:

Blank paper, pencils, and colored pencils

Procedure:

Remind students that the cover is the first thing that the audience will see of their comic books. Therefore, it is important to design an interesting cover, but one that also reflects what the comic book is about. As a demonstration, examine some comic book covers created by professionals or other students. Their covers should represent elements of the comic book, perhaps the characters, settings, or events from the story.

Have students start the cover design in pencil. Once the drawings are complete, then have them color. Then have students think of an appropriate title for the comic book and include it as part of the design. If the comic book is being created by a group of students, they can share the tasks for the cover design as well.

Thought Questions/Discussion Ideas:

1. How does your cover tell the reader what the comic book is about?
2. How did you come up with your title for your comic book?
3. Now that you have finished your comic book, how will you display it for other people?

Extra Activities:

1. Draw a small self-portrait of yourself and put it in a corner of your comic book cover.
2. Re-create your comic book story in musical form through an original song or rap.
3. Create a crossword puzzle, word game, or board game that could be inserted into your comic book.

CLASSROOM RESOURCES

Books related to after-school education or disciplinary learning:

Fashola, O. S. (2002). *Building effective afterschool programs.* Thousand Oaks, CA: Corwin Press.

Noam, G. G., Biancarosa, G., & Dechausay, N. (2002). *Afterschool education: Approaches to an emerging field.* Cambridge, MA: Harvard Education Press.

Wineburg, S., & Grossman, P. (Eds.). (2000). *Interdisciplinary curriculum: Challenges to implementation.* New York: Teachers College Press.

Internet resources related to starting a comic book club:

http://comicsintheclassroom.net/2009/reviews/comicclub.htm
http://graphicclassroom.blogspot.com/2009/06/hall-of-heroes-comic-book-club-for.html
http://www.robertbownefoundation.org/pdf_files/occasional_paper_06.pdf

Comics that relate to specific content areas:

Elementary school level:

Boyd, B. (2005). *The civil rights freedom train.* Williamsburg, VA: Chester Comix.

Selenia Science Comics (http://www.sciencecomics.uwe.ac.uk).

Middle school level:

Ottaviani, J., Cannon, Z., & Cannon, K. (2009). *T-minus: The race to the moon.* New York: Aladdin.

Schultz, M., Cannon, Z., & Cannon, K. (2009). *The stuff of life: A graphic guide to genetics and DNA.* New York: Hill & Wang.

High school level:

Helfer, A., & DuBurke, R. (2007). *Malcolm X: A graphic biography.* New York: Hill & Wang.

Zinn, H., Konopacki, M., & Buhle, P. (2008). *A people's history of American empire.* New York: Metropolitan Books.

Beyond the Words and Art

I t is a curriculum developer's dream to witness the transformation of an idea into a movement that has affected thousands of children world-wide. Of course, I have assumed a role in that process, but it turns out that my greatest strength is knowing when to get out of the way. By turning over a curricular process to teachers, CBP became a showcase for the ability, creativity, and determination of many educators, and the ensuing ability, creativity, and determination of their students. By providing a framework but not dictating the implementation, CBP required teachers to think of themselves as instructional designers. They adopted the project as their own by customizing materials, reshuffling schedules, seeking collaborative opportunities, and developing assessment tools for the sole purpose of meeting the needs of the group of students before them. A textbook or scripted curriculum would never have enabled them to do that.

Moreover, teachers and students alike rediscovered in real time a simple formula that every course in teacher preparation advances, that volumes of research have demonstrated, and that common sense dictates as true: When children are engaged in learning, they learn more. There are numerous strategies in the educational universe for "engaging" young people in learning. Many school districts are paying students with cash, computers, and even cars for better grades. Some suggest jailing young people for truancy, hoping that if the students would only show up to school, learning would follow. Threats to hold children back for poor test scores have been a failed impetus to do better in school. Regardless of the effectiveness of these extrinsic motivators, I do not think I am being naive in advocating the notion that teachers can foster in students a lifelong love of learning *if* the curricula and pedagogies are personally relevant and inspiring of original, creative ideas. With the equivalence of blank paper and some pencils, CBP reinforced the concepts that in student-centered learning children actually do something, in project-based learning they create something, and in inquiry-based learning they ask many questions of themselves and their teachers.

At the heart of all this is creativity, which has been become misunderstood—in fact, politicized—in education. The prevailing notion is that students get creative in music and art class, and then get down to the nuts and bolts of learning in English and math class. This is a falsity on multiple levels. First off, involvement in the arts does not necessitate creative thinking (e.g., playing a scale for intonation or practicing a brush stroke for consistency). More important, however, authentic learning—regardless of content area—revolves around creativity: unique, independent, and original thinking. Our self-imposed dichotomy of creative learning in one classroom and "regular" learning in another is nonsensical. Many educators have discovered through CBP that one does not have to be an artist or art educator to foster creative learning in the arts and literacy. Creative ideas naturally seep across the borders of our constricted content areas, thereby helping teachers and students unearth connections between English and social studies, for example, or science and music.

These lessons learned are not specific to CBP. There are many examples of how creative projects can bolster learning across the content areas. As with the Educational Video Center (Goodman, 2003), Youth Radio (Chavez & Soep, 2005), and another curricular project of mine called the Youth Music Exchange (Bitz, 2009b), digital technology is often a part of the equation. Such new technologies can be a wonderful and resourceful tool, but only that. Without creative thinking, instruction with technology is just as passive as instruction with a textbook. A number of CBP clubs learned this the hard way by plunking students in front of computers loaded with software and images. The youths stared blankly at the screen, just as they would at a piece of paper, before surreptitiously heading over to MySpace and Facebook.

THREE THINGS TO REMEMBER

In closing, I offer three points of advice based on 10 years of observations of successful comic book clubs and, not surprisingly, successful classrooms.

1) Be Flexible

Your first concept of a comic book initiative may not be the best one for your particular group of students. Teachers sometimes misgauge students' excitement about comics or their willingness to try new things. An arsenal of short, quick-paced activities can get the entire class on board, but if one activity falls short, do not dwell on it. Find what works—this may be different from class to class, year to year. A set of lesson plans and planned activities, including those found in each chapter of this book, are useful and likely necessary. But remember the plans are a guide and should not mandate a certain procedure.

2) Build Partnerships

Nobody can accomplish everything on their own, although teachers are often expected to do so. Partnerships create win-win situations for all parties involved, and they enable good ideas to take root and grow in a given school or community. Comic book partnerships can be small, perhaps between like-minded teachers, or large in the collaboration of schools, libraries, funding organizations, and community-based nonprofits. Building a partnership with parents can also be extremely effective—numerous parents have discovered in themselves literacy and artistic abilities that they then parlayed into mentoring opportunities.

3) Listen

Teachers can learn an extraordinary amount about their students' abilities if they listen to the children and then mine what they say for educational activities. An essential part of listening, of course, is establishing opportunities for students to express themselves through words and other media. I will never forget a fourth-grade student in the Bronx who participated in CBP in 2005. He completed his comic book, and his teacher asked him to hand it in so that I could collect it for the website, publication, and exhibit. The student would not let go of the comic. The teacher even began to tug it from his hands. Still he would not let go. Eventually, the teacher and I shrugged at each other and let the student keep his comic book. As we walked away, he said, "This is the only thing that's ever mattered to me." That is a lesson I will never forget.

References

Allen, K., & Ingulsrud, J. E. (2005). Reading manga: Patterns of personal literacies among adolescents. *Language and Education, 19*(4), 265–280.

Allington, A. (2002). *Big Brother and the national reading curriculum: How ideology trumped evidence.* Portsmouth, NH: Heinemann.

Alvermann, D. E., Moon, J. S., & Hagood, M. C. (1999). *Popular culture in the classroom.* Newark, DE: International Reading Association.

American Library Association. (2008). *Dealing with challenges to graphic novels.* Retrieved October 13, 2009, from www.ala.org/Template.cfm?Section= ifissues&Template=/ContentManagement/ContentDisplay.cfm& ContentID=130336

Anderson, H., & Styles, M. (1999). *Teaching through texts: Promoting literacy through popular and literary texts in the primary classroom.* New York: Routledge.

Barbanel, J. (1994, March 24). Gunfire kills two students after fight at a Bronx park. *New York Times.* Retrieved October 13, 2009, from http://www.nytimes. com/1994/03/24/nyregion/gunfire-kills-two-students-after-fight-at-a-bronx-park.html

Bartlet, D. (2005). The sketchbook as artist's book. *School Arts, 104*(9), 34.

Barton, J., & Sawyer, D. M. (2003). Our students are ready for this: Comprehension instruction in the elementary school. *The Reading Teacher, 57*, 322–333.

Beylie, C. (1964, September). Are comics an art? *Lettres et Médecins*, pp. 9–29.

Bitz, M. (2004a). The Comic Book Project: Forging alternative pathways to literacy. *Journal of Adolescent & Adult Literacy, 47*(7), 574–586.

Bitz, M. (2004b). The Comic Book Project: The lives of urban youth. *Art Education, 57*(2), 33–39.

Bitz, M. (2006). The art of democracy/Democracy as art: Creative learning in after-school comic book clubs. *Afterschool Matters Occasional Papers Series, 7*, 1–20.

Bitz, M. (2008a). The Comic Book Project: Literacy outside (and inside) the box. In J. Flood, S. B. Heath, & D. Lapp (Eds.), *Handbook of Research on Teaching Literacy through the Communicative and Visual Arts* (Vol. 2, pp. 229–236). New York: Erlbaum.

Bitz. M. (2008b). A rare bridge: The Comic Book Project connects learning with life. *Teachers & Writers, 39*(4), 2–13.

Bitz, M. (2009a). *Manga High: Literacy, identity, and coming of age in an urban high school.* Cambridge, MA: Harvard Education Press.

Bitz, M. (2009b). The Tupac Effect: A case for socially relevant education. In M. Hagood (Ed.), *New literacies practices: Designing literacy learning* (pp. 7–24). New York: Peter Lang.

Black, R. W. (2005). Access and affiliation: The literacy and composition practices of English-language learners in an online fanfiction community. *Journal of Adolescent & Adult Literacy, 49*(2), 118–128.

Bond, S. J., & Hayes, J. R. (1984). Cues people use to paragraph text. *Research in the Teaching of English, 18*(2), 147–167.

Booth, D., & Lundy, K. (2007). *Boosting literacy with graphic novels.* Orlando, FL: Steck-Vaughn.

Broome, J., & Kane, G. (1959). *Green Lantern: Featuring "Menace of the runaway missile."* New York: DC Comics.

Bruner, J. (1986). *Actual minds, possible worlds.* Cambridge, MA: Harvard University Press.

Bucher, K. T., & Manning, M. L. (2004). Bringing graphic novels into a school's curriculum. *Clearing House, 78*(2), 67.

Buckingham, D. (Ed.). (1998). *Teaching popular culture: Beyond radical pedagogy.* London: UCL Press.

Buckingham, D. (2003). Media education and the end of the critical consumer. *Harvard Educational Review, 73*(3), 309–327.

Calkins, L. (1986). *The art of teaching writing.* Portsmouth, NH: Heinemann.

Calkins, L. (1994). *The art of teaching writing* (New ed.). Portsmouth, NH: Heinemann.

Calkins, L. (2003). *Nuts and bolts of teaching writing.* Portsmouth, NH: Heinemann.

Cambourne, B. (2002). Holistic, integrated approaches to reading and language arts instruction: The constructivist framework of an instructional theory. In A. E. Farstrup & S. J. Samuels (Eds.), *What research has to say about reading instruction* (3rd ed., pp. 25–47). Newark, DE: International Reading Association.

Canudo, R. (1923). Manifesto of the seven arts. *Literature/Film Quarterly* [1975], *3*(3), 252–254.

Carter, J. (Ed.). (2007). *Building literacy connections with graphic novels: Page by page, panel by panel.* Urbana, IL: National Council of Teachers of English.

Carter, J. B. (2009). [Review of the book *Manga High: Literacy, identity, and comic of age in an urban high school*]. *Journal of Youth and Adolescence.* DOI 10.1007/s10964-009-9443-7.

Cary, S. (2004). *Going graphic: Comics at work in the multilingual classroom.* Portsmouth, NH: Heinemann.

Castellucci, C., & Rugg, J. (2007). *The plain Janes.* New York: Minx.

Chandler-Olcott, K. (2008). Anime and manga fandom: Young people's multiliteracies made visible. In J. Flood, S. B. Heath, & D. Lapp (Eds.), *Handbook of research on teaching literacy through the communicative and visual arts* (Vol. 2, pp. 247–257). New York: Erlbaum.

Chavez, V., & Soep, L. (2005). Youth Radio and the pedagogy of collegiality. *Harvard Education Review, 75*(4), 409–434.

Chilcoat, G. W. (1993). Teaching about the civil rights movement by using student-generated comic books. *Social Studies, 84,* 113–118.

City, E. A., Elmore, R. F., Fiarman, S. E., & Teitel, L. (2009). *Instructional rounds in education: A network approach to improving teaching and learning.* Cambridge, MA: Harvard Education Press.

Clapp, E. R. (1939). *Community schools in action*. New York: Arno Press.

Collins, J. L. (1998). *Strategies for struggling writers*. New York: Guilford.

Condon, M. W., & McGuffee, M. (2001). *Real epublishing, really publishing! How to create digital books by and for all ages*. Portsmouth, NH: Heinemann.

Crawford, P. (2004). A novel approach: Using graphic novels to attract reluctant readers and promote literacy. *Library Media Connection, 22*(5), 26.

Cummins, J. (2003). Reading and the bilingual student: Fact and friction. In G. Garcia (Ed.), *English learners: Reaching the highest level of English literacy* (pp. 2–33). Newark, DE: International Reading Association.

Decker, L. E. (1972). *Foundations of community education*. Midland, MI: Pendell.

Densel, S. (2005). All together now: A district-wide mural project. *SchoolArts, 105*(4), 35–37.

DeSimone, B. (2006). Drawing on justice. *Teaching Tolerance* (online). Retrieved October 13, 2009, from http://www.tolerance.org/teach/magazine/features.jsp?p=0&is=38&ar=644#

Dewey, J. (1916). *Democracy and education*. New York: Macmillan.

Dewey, J. (1998). *Experience and education*. Indianapolis: Kappa Delta Pi.

Dorrell, L. D. (1987). Why comic books? *School Library Journal, 34*(3), 30–32.

Dorrell, L. D., & Carroll, C. E. (1981). Spider-Man at the library. *School Library Journal, 27*(10), 17–19.

Drooker, E. (2002a). *Blood song: A silent ballad*. New York: Harcourt.

Drooker, E. (2002b). *Flood! A novel in pictures* (2nd ed.). Milwaukee, OR: Dark Horse.

Dyson, A. H. (1993). *Social worlds of children learning to write in an urban primary school*. New York: Teachers College Press.

Dyson, A. H. (1997). *Writing superheroes: Contemporary childhood, popular culture, and classroom literacy*. New York: Teachers College Press.

Dyson, A. H. (2003). *The brothers and sisters learn to write: Popular literacies in childhood and school cultures*. New York: Teachers College Press.

Duffy, R. (1994). It's just like talking to each other: Written conversation with 5-year-old children. In N. Hall & A. Robinson (Eds.), *Keeping in touch: Using interactive writing with young children* (pp. 31–42). Portsmouth, NH: Heinemann.

Efland, A. (2002). *Art and cognition: Integrating the visual arts in the curriculum*. New York: Teachers College Press.

Eilers, L. H., & Pinkley, C. (2006). Metacognitive strategies help students to comprehend all text. *Reading Improvement, 43*(1), 13–29.

Eisner, E. (2002). *The arts and the creation of mind*. New Haven, CT: Yale University Press.

Eisner, W. (1985). *Comics and sequential art*. Tamarac, FL: Poorhouse Press.

Eisner, W. (1996). *Graphic storytelling and visual narrative*. Tamarac, FL: Poorhouse Press.

Elbow, J. (2002). The role of publication in the democratization of writing. In C. Weber (Ed.), *Publishing with students: A comprehensive guide (1–8)*. Portsmouth, NH: Heinemann.

Fillmore, L. W., & Valdez, C. (1986). Teaching bilingual learners. In M. E. Wittrock (Ed.), *Handbook of research on teaching* (pp. 648–685). New York: Macmillan.

Fitzgerald, J. (1989). Research on stories: Implications for teachers. In K. P. Muth (Ed.), *Children's comprehension of text: Research into practice* (pp. 2–36). Newark, DE: International Reading Association.

Flood, J., Heath, S. B., & Lapp, D. (Eds.). (1997). *Handbook of research on teaching literacy through the communicative and visual arts* (Vol. 1). New York: Macmillan.

Flood, J., Heath, S. B., & Lapp, D. (Eds.). (2008). *Handbook of research on teaching literacy through the communicative and visual arts* (Vol. 2). New York: Erlbaum.

Frey, N., & Fisher, D. (Eds.). (2008). *Teaching visual literacy: Using comic books, graphic novels, anime, cartoons, and more to develop comprehension and thinking skills.* Thousand Oaks, CA: Corwin Press.

Fry, E. B. (1968). A readability formula that saves time. *Journal of Reading, 11*(7), 513–516.

Gardner, H. (1983, 1993). *Frames of mind: The theory of multiple intelligences.* New York: Basic Books.

Gentry, J. (2008). E-publishing's impact on learning in an inclusive sixth grade social studies classroom. *Journal of Interactive Learning Research, 19*(3), 455–467.

Goldman, S. R., Saul, E. U., & Coté, N. (1995). Paragraphing, reader, and task effects on discourse comprehension. *Discourse Processes, 20,* 273–305.

Goldstein, B. S. (1986). Looking at cartoons and comics in a new way. *Journal of Reading, 29*(7), 657–661.

Goodman, S. (2003). *Teaching youth media.* New York: Teachers College Press.

Gorman, M. (2003). *Getting graphic: Using graphic novels to promote literacy with preteens and teens.* Columbus, OH: Linworth.

Grace, D., & Tobin, J. (1998). Butt jokes and mean-teacher parodies: Video production in the elementary classroom. In D. Buckingham (Ed.), *Teaching popular culture: Beyond radical pedagogy* (pp. 42–62): London: UCL Press.

Graves, D. H. (1975). Examination of the writing processes of seven-year-old children. *Research in the Teaching of English, 9,* 221–241.

Graves, D. H. (1983). *Writing: Teachers and children at work.* Exeter, NH: Heinemann.

Guilford, J. A. (1965). *Fundamental statistics in psychology and education* (4th ed.). New York: McGraw-Hill.

Gunning, T. (2006). *Closing the literacy gap.* Boston: Allyn & Bacon.

Gurney, H. G. (2008). Community friendship fence mural. *SchoolArts, 108*(4), 38–39.

Guzzetti, B. J., & Gamboa, M. (2004). Zines for social justice: Adolescent girls writing on their own. *Reading Research Quarterly, 39*(4), 408–436.

Hansen, J. (2004). *"Tell me a story": Developmentally appropriate retelling strategies.* Newark, DE: International Reading Association.

Harste, J. C., Short, K. G., & Burke, C. (1988). *Creating classrooms for authors: The reading-writing connection.* Portsmouth, NH: Heinemann.

Hata, K. (2008). *Hayate, the combat butler.* New York: Viz Media.

Hayes, D., & Ahrens, M. (1988). Vocabulary simplification for children: A special case of "motherese"? *Journal of Child Language, 15,* 395–410.

Heer, J., & Worcester, K. (Eds.). (2009). *A comics studies reader.* Jackson: University Press of Mississippi.

Hennessey, J., & McConnell, A. (2008). *The United States Constitution: A graphic adaptation*. New York: Hill & Wang.

Hetland, L., Winner, E., Veenema, S., & Sheridan, K. M. (2007). *Studio thinking: The real benefits of visual arts education*. New York: Teachers College Press.

Heyer, Z. L. (2009). The students are the living authors: Publishing student work using print on demand. *English Journal, 98*(3), 59–65.

House, E. R., & Howe, K. R. (2000). Deliberative democratic evaluation. In K. E. Ryan & L. DeStefano (Eds.), *Evaluation as a democratic process: Promoting inclusion, dialogue, and deliberation* (pp. 3–12). San Francisco: Jossey-Bass.

Imperial County Office of Education. (2009). *Supplemental report on student performance data*. El Centro, CA: Author.

Inhelder, B., & Piaget, J. (1958). *The growth of logical thinking from childhood to adolescence*. New York: Basic.

James, H. (1986). *The portrait of a lady*. London: Penguin.

Kellner, D. (1998). Multiple literacies and critical pedagogy. *Educational Theory, 48*(1), 103–122.

Khurana, S. (2005). So you want to be a superhero? How the art of making comics in an afterschool setting can develop young people's creativity, literacy, and identity. *Afterschool Matters, 4*, 1–9.

Kincaid, J. P., Fishburne, R. P., Rogers, R. L., & Chissom, B. S. (1975). Derivation of new readability formulas (Automated Readability Index, Fog Count and Flesch Reading Ease Formula) for navy enlisted personnel. *Research Branch Report, 8*(75). Millington, TN: Naval Technical Training, U.S. Naval Air Station, Memphis, TN.

Kirker, S. S. (2007). Magnificent clay murals. *SchoolArts, 107*(2), 26–27.

Krashen, S. (2004). *The power of reading: Insights from the research* (2nd ed.). Santa Barbara, CA: Libraries Unlimited.

Lensmire, T. (1994). *When children write: Critical re-visions of the writing workshop*. New York: Teachers College Press.

Lowenfeld, V. (1947). *Creative and mental growth*. New York: Macmillan.

MacDonald, H. (2004). Drawing a crowd: Graphic novel events are great ways to generate excitement. *School Library Journal, 50*(8), S20.

Manchel, F. (1990). *Film study: An analytical bibliography* (Vol. 4). Madison, NJ: Farleigh Dickinson University Press.

Martin, G. (1997). *The art of comic book inking*. Milwaukie, WI: Dark Horse Comics.

McCloud, S. (1993). *Understanding comics: The invisible art*. New York: Harper-Collins.

McCloud, S. (2009). *The "Infinite Canvas."* Retrieved October 13, 2009, from http://scottmccloud.com/4-inventions/canvas/index.html

Merrill, B. T. (2008). From mission statement to murals. *SchoolArts, 108*(4), 38–39.

Michaelis, D. (2007). *Schulz and Peanuts: A biography*. New York: HarperCollins.

Moore, A., & Gibbons, D. (1986). *Watchmen*. New York: DC Comics.

Morrison, T., Bryan, G., & Chilcoat, G. (2002). Using student-generated comic books in the classroom. *Journal of Adolescent & Adult Literacy, 45*(8), 758–767.

Mouly, F. (2009). Foreword. In M. Bitz, *Manga High: Literacy, identity, and coming of age in an urban high school* (pp. ix–xii). Cambridge, MA: Harvard Education Press.

Muschla, G. R. (1993). *Writing workshop survival kit.* West Nyack, NY: Center for Applied Research in Education.

National Commission on Writing. (2006). *Writing and school reform (including the neglected "R").* New York: College Board.

NCTE/IRA. (1996). *Standards for the English Language Arts.* Urbana, IL: National Council of Teachers of English.

New York State Department of Education. (1996). *New York State learning standards for English language arts.* Retrieved January 26, 2009, from http://www.emsc.nysed.gov/ciai/ela/pub/elalearn.pdf

Nodelman, P. (1988). *Words about pictures: The narrative art of children's picture books.* Athens: University of Georgia Press.

Nyberg, A. K. (1998). *Seal of approval: The history of the Comics Code.* Jackson: University Press of Mississippi.

O'English, L., Matthews, J. G., & Lindsay, E. B. (2006). Graphic novels in academic libraries: From "Maus" to manga and beyond. *Journal of Academic Librarianship, 32*(2), 173–182.

Ogle, D. M. (1989). The know, want to know, learn strategy. In K. D. Muth (Ed.), *Children's comprehension of text* (pp. 205–223). Newark, DE: International Reading Association.

Parsons, M. J. (1987). *How we understand art: A cognitive development account of aesthetic experience.* Cambridge: Cambridge University Press.

Perkins, J. H. (2008). *Why our schools need the arts.* New York: Teachers College Press.

Prokop, C. (2007). The team approach to art. *SchoolArts, 108*(3), 24–25.

Reid, C. (2007). New report finds manga sales up; Anime DVD down in '07. *Publishers Weekly* (online). Retrieved October 13, 2009, from http://www.publishersweekly.com/article/CA6510598.html

Ritchie, D. A. (2003). *Doing oral history: A practical guide.* Oxford, UK: Oxford University Press.

Rolheiser, C. (Ed.). (1996). *Self-evaluation . . . Helping students get better at it!* Ajax, ON: Visutronx.

Routman, R. (2000). *Conversations.* Portsmouth, NH: Heinemann.

Satrapi, M. (2003). *Persepolis: The story of a childhood.* New York: Pantheon.

Scardamalia, M., & Bereiter, C. (1986). Research on written composition. In M. C. Wittrock (Ed.), *Handbook of Research on Teaching* (pp. 778–863). New York: Macmillan.

Schwarcz, J. (1982). *Ways of the illustrator: Visual communication in children's literature.* Chicago: American Library Association.

Schwartz, A., & Rubinstein-Avila, E. (2006). Understanding the manga hype: Uncovering the multimodality of comic-book literacies. *Journal of Adolescent & Adult Literacy, 50*(1), 40–49.

Sexton, A., & Pantoja, T. (2008). *Shakespeare's "Hamlet": The manga edition.* Hoboken, NJ: Wiley.

Sfar, J. (2006). *Vampire loves.* New York: First Second Books.

Sheridan, S. R. (1997). *Drawing/writing and the new literacy.* Amherst, MA: Drawing/Writing.

Siegel, M. (1995). More than words: The generative power of transmediation for learning. *Canadian Journal of Education, 20,* 455–475.

Simons, H. D., & Ammon, P. (1989). Child knowledge and primerese text: Mismatches and miscues. *Research in the Teaching of English, 23*(4), 380–398.

Sipe, L. (2008). *Storytime: Young children's literary understanding in the classroom.* New York: Teachers College Press.

Smith, J. (2005). *Bone.* New York: Scholastic.

Snow, C. E., Burns, M. S., & Griffin, P. (1998). *Preventing reading difficulties in young children.* Washington, DC: National Academy Press.

Spandel, V. (2001). *Creating writers through 6-trait writing assessment and instruction.* New York: Longman.

Spiegelman, A. (2003). *The complete Maus.* New York: Penguin.

Stadler, M. A., & Ward, G. C. (2005). Supporting the narrative development of young children. *Early Childhood Education Journal, 33*(2), 73–80.

Stern, R. (1984). *The Mighty Avengers: The Vision takes command!* New York: Marvel Comics.

Strickland, D. S. (1988). Educating African American learners at risk: Finding a better way. In C. Weaver (Ed.), *Practicing what we know: Informed reading instruction* (pp. 394–408). Urbana, IL: National Council of Teachers of English.

Suhor, C. (1984). Towards a semiotics-based curriculum. *Journal of Curriculum Studies, 16,* 247–257.

Sulzby, E. (1992). Transitions from emergent to conventional writing: Research directions. *Language Arts, 68,* 50–57.

Sulzby, E., Barnhart, J., & Hieshima, J. (1989). *Forms of writing and rereading from writing: A preliminary report* (Technical Report No. 20). Berkeley: University of California, Center for the Study of Writing.

Szymusiak, K., & Sibberson, F. (2001). *Beyond leveled books: Supporting transitional readers in grades 2–5.* York, ME: Stenhouse.

Thomas, J. L. (1983). *Cartoons and comics in the classroom: A reference for teachers and librarians.* Littleton, CO: Libraries Unlimited.

Timber Frame. (2003). *Comic book Shakespeare: Macbeth.* London: Author.

Tulenko, J. (2009, March 31). Schools cope with rising numbers of homeless students. *NewsHour.* Retrieved October 13, 2009, from http://www.pbs.org/newshour/bb/business/jan-june09/schoolhomeless_03-31.html

Tunnel, M. O., & Jacobs, J. S. (1989). Using real books: Research findings on literature-based reading instruction. *Reading Teacher, 42*(7), 470–477.

U.S. Congress. (1955). *Comic books and juvenile delinquency: Interim report pursuant to S. Res. 89, 83d Cong., 1st sess., and S. 190, 83d Cong., 2d sess., a part of the investigation of juvenile delinquency in the United States.* Washington, DC: U.S. Government Printing Office.

Versaci, R. (2007). *This book contains graphic language: Comics as literature.* London: Continuum.

Vygotsky, L. S. (1978). *Thought and language.* Cambridge: MIT Press.

Wertham, F. (1954). *Seduction of the innocent.* New York: Rinehart.

Wilson, B. (1988). The artistic tower of Babel: Inextricable links between culture and graphic development. In G. W. Hardman & T. Zernich (Eds.), *Discerning art: Concepts and issues* (pp. 488–506). Champaign, IL: Stipes.

Wilson, B. (1999). Becoming Japanese: Manga, children's drawings, and the construction of national character. *Visual Arts Research, 25*(2), 48–60.

Wolk, D. (2008). *Reading comics: How graphic novels work and what they mean.* New York: Da Capo.

Wright, G. (1979). The comic book: A forgotten medium in the classroom. *Reading Teacher, 33,* 158–161.

Wright, G., & Sherman, R. (1999). Let's create a comic strip. *Reading Improvement, 36*(2), 66–72.

Yang, G. L. (2006). *American born Chinese.* New York: First Second Books.

Yuill, N., & Oakhill, J. (1991). *Children's problems in text comprehension: An experimental investigation* (Cambridge Monographs & Texts in Applied Psycholinguistics). New York: Cambridge University Press.

Index

About the Author

Dr. Michael Bitz, EdD, is the executive director of the Center for Educational Pathways (www.edpath.org), a nonprofit organization that establishes creative pathways to academic success for underserved youth. He is the first recipient of the Educational Entrepreneurship Fellowship at the Mind Trust in Indianapolis, and he received the Distinguished Alumni Early Career Award from Teachers College, Columbia University. Dr. Bitz is the founder of the Comic Book Project and cofounder of the Youth Music Exchange, innovative curricula that have reached children worldwide and have been featured by the *New York Times*, *Washington Post*, Associated Press, National Public Radio, and many others. Dr. Bitz has served on the faculty of Teachers College, Columbia University; Manhattanville College; and Ramapo College.